EOD 5174

P9-EDF-177

C10/2 op 73

RENEWALS 691-4574

WITHDRAWN
UTSA LIBRARIES

WHISPERS

Also by B. H. Friedman

fiction
CIRCLES (1962)
YARBOROUGH (1964)

non-fiction
SCHOOL OF NEW YORK: Some Younger Artists (edited and
introduced, 1959)
ROBERT GOODNOUGH (with Barbara Guest, 1962)
LEE KRASNER (1965)
JACKSON POLLOCK: Energy Made Visible (1972)
ALFONSO OSSORIO (1972)

Words, words, words. . . Hamlet must have been reading a novel.

The Temptation to Exist   E.M. Cioran

Money is a kind of poetry.

Adagia   Wallace Stevens

WHISPERS
B. H. Friedman

an ithaca house book
Ithaca, New York

Portions of this book appeared in *the noble savage 4, New American Review 5* and *Shankpainter 5.*

Cover design: Dennis Potokar

Copyright, 1972, by B. H. Friedman
Ithaca House, 314 Forest Home Drive
Ithaca, New York, 14850

I S B N 0-87886-021-5

All rights reserved. No part of this book may be reproduced without written permission of the publishers except for brief excerpts in reviews.

LIBRARY
University of Texas
At San Antonio

ITHACA HOUSE
314 Forest Home Drive
Ithaca, New York
14850

For Nancy and Jim Dine

WHISPERS

wHISpers
wHispERS
wHISpers
wHispERS
wHISpers
wHispERS
wHISpers
wHispERS
wHISpers
wHispERS
wHISpers
wHispERS

wHISpers
wHispERS
wHISpers
wHispERS
wHISpers
wHispERS
wHISpers
wHispERS
wHISpers
wHispERS
wHISpers
wHispERS
wHISpers

Part One
(the 'fifties and early 'sixties)

his: #1

Can you hear me?

The New York I love is so cool you may not recognize
her. Cooler than the neon at Times Square. Cooler than the
drinks at Yankee Stadium. Cooler than the snow in Harlem.
It's cool near the top.

I love what critics hate: executive dining rooms of Wall
Street banks, big legal offices with rows of CCH reports, the
patterns made by teleregisters, and the way necktie stripes
move up to the left among men who move to the right. The
towers should be connected by bridges. I go down only to re-
fuel—i.e., when not eating at some cloudy club. Down there,
I like those filling stations in the mid-forties—Christ Cella,
Pietro's, the Palm, places where they cut meat the thickness
of lumber—and the French ones farther north where fish swim
in sauce. . . . I like them because the food is good and cheaper
than the places that cost money. New York is almost free, if
you love your work. (Once I saw a guy ask a cab driver for
a receipt.)

The skyline's free. I like leaving the city and returning
to it by air. The city planners haven't been able to organize
the air. I like the top of the G. E. building, as visible from the
garden behind our brownstone house as are the chandeliers by
Louis Comfort Tiffany in the windows of Second Avenue
antique shops. I wish Comfort were my middle name.

I'm too well dressed to go into Third Avenue bars; my
clothes are always picking fights with people. (Are my lapels
as narrow as piping?) I miss the protective shadows of the el.
The guys are right who look in garbage cans, if they don't
have to. They're painters or poets or businessmen. I like
everything disposable. Cigarettes, whiskey, newspapers, soap,
candy bars, razor blades—those are the businesses to be in.
Imagine going to bed each night with the knowledge that you
have packaged people's desires, that you have given them that
sense of reality only waste can give. I like art before it goes
into museums. I like a city that can throw away the Ritz with-
out batting an eye (and then sell its elevator cabs to Texas oil-
men to convert into ranch-style bars). I like what's in paren-
theses, too, more than seeing those same cabs sold to Holly-
wood as lampbases. If life is a choice between lampbases and
bars, I choose bars because they remind me of parentheses. If
life is a choice. . . .
     I like the papers I see on businessmen's desks: Dun &
Bradstreet reports ("Credit is Man's Confidence in Man"),
Proudfoot, Dodge, Standard and Poor's, Moody's. Moody I
like best of all. I wish Moody were my last name. I picture
him as he must have been: a beard. The others all sound as
though they knew exactly what they were doing. I like letter-
heads, trademarks, logotypes. I like statements of income and
expense—outcome: black ink. I like black ink. I like analyses
of projected earnings; inventories; contracts; licenses; per-
mits; legal documents of all kinds, especially those in pale
blue binders. Getting and spending we lay waste our money.
I like the printed literature that comes from trade associations.
I don't forget it wasn't always printed. I don't forget the ten-
der New York girls who took it down in Pitman or Gregg.
Take me down, gently, gently, as you would a word.

I like the sad world of the wastepaper basket. I like the cleaning ladies who give office buildings that arbitrarily illuminated look at night. Seagram is wrong. Uniform elegance is wrong. Waste can't be that well organized. Oh, that blue light at the top of the G. E. building—more than arbitrary, a surprise, a displaced star. I wish it hung in my home. Again I wish Comfort were my middle name, and Moody my last. I wish I had a first name instead of initials.

What else goes on at night besides the lights? The music. You've got to be crazy to pass a law forbidding people to blow their horns. I hate low quiet cities. I like it up high where the hum bounces between Rockefeller Center and Wall Street. I like, too, those sterling phoenixes of the boom, the Empire State and Chrysler buildings. (I want to think the latter was named for a violinist who hit high notes: a monumental misspelling.) I like thin air. I make exceptions sometimes, plunge downstairs into smoke, and usually regret it. Hell went underground in the 'fifties (like everyone was digging like). I prefer places where you can walk straight in: the Half Note, say, if you can get a cab to go to Hudson Street. I like Hudson. I like his river. The wild ones with the Indian names all belong to Thomas Wolfe. This one belongs to us. A tame tender river with nothing but a destination. It's just kind of there to say hello to, like Santa Claus outside of Macy's at Christmas. The East River's tame and tender too. It's just kind of there to say hello to, like Santa Claus outside of Bloomingdale's at Christmas. To the distant sound of bells and horns, these rivers embrace us.

New York has two seasons now, according to the engineers. There's that foggy time during the summer that makes me want to try haiku:

Moon rain
air-conditions
New York streets
Or:
New York
moon rain
from air-conditioners
Or:
Air-conditioners
moon rain
New York

(No matter how I turn these phrases—typically, towards the sun—they will not fatten into traditional haiku: I need a briefer form.)

And there's that steamy time in winter, when verse forms become still more difficult (begging for still more missing syllables), and you can't get tickets to anything, and the stores (even the little ones upstairs) are crowded. Smoking a cigar after lunch, I watch other executives ice-skating; they wear pin-striped suits and scarves and gloves. New York is a Japanese Egyptian etcetera kind of place. All the different newspapers and magazines at Hotalings. All the different kinds of cars in showrooms. When are the Russians going to build a good sports car? I want to drive a fast car to the moon. I want to touch the real moon rain.

I like invisible voices, frequency-modulated voices. I like the idea that people who sleep during the day can get the commercials at night.

There's nothing on Broadway except a few good movies that will reach your neighborhood playhouse. (My neighborhood playhouse is my bed; my living room is my bedroom; the

TV's so close I can touch it.) There's not much off Broadway either. The best plays are being made in bed—or never get produced. I hate the whole theater-concert-prison situation. I want to drink and smoke and move around. The best thing about theater is the intermission. I like the furs and cigarette holders. I like that particular draft which enters lobbies in the West Forties. I like the dash to the nearest bar. I like the Rolls with the blue lamp up on top.

I like the hearses that even the cabbies respect. I hope I leave town tying up traffic, on my way to suburbs so full of cemeteries they can bury everybody horizontally even though the efficiency experts recommend vertically.

Efficiency experts! Experts of all kinds! Business is a world of delights I cannot afford in the other world, the world of home. This is my home, my recaptured childhood, where chairs swivel and roll around on little wheels, where I have two telephones on my desk, where the drawers slide out on runners (never too far), where the bar in the executive conference room has an executive refrigerator with an executive ice tray in which there's *always* enough executive ice, etc. I have a secretary who frees me for business and from bills, personal income tax forms, wife presents, dealings with garage mechanics, watch repairmen, G.E. (in the other home everything breaks). Just a phone call for shirts or underwear or socks: always the same. She can buy my anonymity from haberdashers as others buy their identity. My identity is my anonymity. I don't exist away from my office, except in other people's offices. I adore this girl who understands the subtleties of a *Who's Who* questionnaire, who understands a thousand subtleties I can't understand:

"Put Mr. A. on. Mr. B. is waiting."

I'm Mr. B.—I'm not waiting.

I'm not waiting, but I'm awed. O my secretary, my lovely machine, you are the subject of my book as I am the subject of yours, that stenographic pad you hold on your knee. I depend on your racing efficient fingers, as you depend on my voice, as a mirror depends on the transient image it holds. . . Take a letter: *Dear. . .*

There are messengers waiting to be shot in any direction. And there's a supply closet—toy closet, I almost said—full of rubberbands and clips and rulers and staples and machines for writing (the French call them) and machines for adding and machines for dictating and machines for duplicating— luxuries, like nonsmudge carbon paper. At home, what have I to compare with these? What have I to fill the time? A wife, children, a house. Nothing. At home I have myself. Evenings, holidays, weekends I must manufacture the irritations that are mine, free, at the office. At home there's always the possibility that the decision may be important. At business the important thing is to decide.

I have decided, like a certain kind of artist (the artist as speculative businessman), to bet on the future. Contrary to popular belief (my secretary's phrase—I adore her, I adore her), New York doesn't exist in the present. It doesn't exist. It is becoming. It is the future. It is aims, plans, preconceptions, projects, means. It is my city, the city of tomorrow's sale. I'll find myself here. There's no time now, but I have forever. (I say this, looking straight ahead, across the street, into the windows of another office. I'm afraid to look down).

The cool nerveless city planners look down. They don't see us, but they, too, see the future—in statistics, traffic and population trends. . . We're nothing. We're the six or seven zeros. We're what they buzz *their* secretaries for, if and when they want us.

Money talks quietly, like me. It's all zeros. Duels now are fought with zeros. The best tables are bought with zeros. The best seats are bought with zeros. Money whispers. Bills no longer crackle in the hands of a headwaiter or a cop. Power used to be noisy. Not now. Now typewriters are silent. Now carpets are thick. Now acoustical tile (simulating travertine) soaks up sound everywhere. And, even in the general offices, vinyl has replaced asphalt; it's quieter, and easier on the feet of clerks who wear sponge-rubber soles so thick one hardly hears them take their coffee breaks. For them, the day is all soft, silent foods, a mush of doughnuts and danish and coffee, mid-morning and mid-afternoon. At lunch they have hamburgers and ice cream, while I chew glass. They're not yet rich enough to chew.

Zeros! And less than zeros: minus quantities. Deducttions. Everything's deductible. I'm deductible. Cocteau, I think it was, remarked, that for the poet $2 + 2 = 5$. For the corporation $2 + 2 = 3$. There seem to be twelve men sitting around the conference table. There are only eleven; one gets lost, ground up among the cigar butts. Everyone has a hand on the wheel of the steering committee. It can't move. Sub-sub-sub-sub a committee down to one, and there's hope. Two minds are worse than one. The corporation is always equal to less than the sum of its parts, and those parts are always equal to less than the sum of their parts. What's good for General Motors (or Electric or Telephone) may be lousy for me. I'm better than my corporate identity. I'm better than my public image. I'm better than the exact fraction I represent of my club, staff, nation, bureau, organization. . . I'm better in indirect proportion to the number of people who shape me in a given situation. I'm better anonymous. I'm better as nothing. I'm better as zero than minus one.

It's quiet. The whisper you hear is air rushing through sheet-metal ducts, hissing its snake-song, forever: 72° F., 50% relative humidity. The air is filtered. The seasons are filtered. The engineers are wrong. There's *one* season. If nature's quarterly dividend is dead, her semi-annual dividend is dying. . . A perfect day is a state of mind, a day in which a deal is made, *the day* in *the season*.

So no "summer" reading for me. What do I read, away from the office? It doesn't matter much. Anything that will fit in my pocket. Anything that will replace the ringing of the office phone. At LaGuardia I pick up Roger Shattuck's *The Banquet Years*, a reprint, of course; I'm always a few years behind. My secretary reads the current books for me (just as she sees the new movies, and I watch the old ones on TV). I read about yesterday. Doing that makes New York possible. Thesis: tomorrow. Antithesis: yesterday. Synthesis: now, an illusion. *The Banquet Years:* about the birth of the avant garde before the avant garde went into business. Hell, three big banquets in thirty years (for Rousseau, Apollinaire, and Saint-Pol-Roux)! I'm invited to three a week at grand ballrooms, one grander than the next. Was fun half as much fun before it became a business? Shattuck says, "The most notable artistic figures of the Banquet Years practiced external non-conformity in order to attain a conformity within the individual." I practice external conformity in order to attain a non-conformity within myself. If tension builds, I turn it into words. Better than letting it become ulcers or cancer. Cancer: the big *C*, not to be confused with the small *c's* in cardiac, or that other little one plunged like a hook into the center of ulcer.

Everything works. Nothing is wasted. Would it have made any difference if I had read something else? All I wanted was an irritant to substitute for the phone, the air-conditioning. . . Odd, the shock sometimes when, precisely at six, the air-conditioning stops. Like any businessman, it's at times like these (evenings, weekends) I find my theme. A journal entry:

It is Sunday. My wife and children have gone to the country. I am left with silence. The silence is my leisure. I don't know what to do with it. I listen. I hear it, the silence, rushing by like air, like the air in air-conditioning ducts. There is no balance to the silence, no calm, no poise—only pressure. This silence, this luxury, this leisure begs insistently to be enjoyed—and destroyed. Finally, I scream. For a few seconds, during the scream, it is quiet, and then the noise begins again.

Appreciate whispers. Two cars collide at an intersection. It's a beautiful sound, but what does it mean?

The sixties so far have been my season in heaven. Will the late sixties be greater yet? The seventies? Up, up into the highest cholesterol. Up, up into the highest brow. Fat will be fashionable. Baldness will be fashionable. The moon will continue to be fashionable. There'll be souped-up elevators in office buildings. There'll be souped-up office buildings in outer space. All soups will be cool and chic: gazpacho, vichyssoisse, infinity. Everyone will have his bowl of infinity. There'll be second helpings of infinity. Just tell the waiter, quietly, you want *more*. The coolness of it all, the endless whispers of it all send endless shivers up my endless spine. Up, up to the ears. I can hardly hear me.

his: #2

The words are more tired now. I'm to go on vacation.

Each year or so I do that—that's done to me. Each year my efficiency at the office reaches a peak which embarrasses everyone. They send me away to slow me down. I have, after all, become so efficient— I have concentrated so hard on my work—that I hardly have time to appreciate the office environment: its pure hard air-conditioned fluorescent seasonless beauty. They say I need a rest.

I face my vacation bravely, as I would the bore of a gun. What's a month's death, if they will let me return? A month, thirty days, twenty-four hours a day, every day, traveling with my wife and without secretary, executive lunches, clubs, lawyers, accountants. . . without reports of their golf scores, their bridge hands—their lusts, in short. I turn the sabbatical cheek.

The other possibility doesn't exist: to send them away, to stay in New York, which I love. New York, the monkey on my back. A month's exile, a month's withdrawal. . . I have only a few weeks in which to make up my mind, in which to select my prison.

At our elevator landing, distinguishable because it is decorated with photographs of our product, I touch DOWN. The plastic mechanism, responding to the heat of my index finger, blushes red. A moment later there's a *musique concrète* ping, and the doors of an elevator spring open. . . Down, down, down. . . I race across the terrazzo in the lobby, defying its slipperiness. I spin through a revolving door. I hail a cab. I say where I'm going (not ultimately, but now). I overtip. I am absolutely, existentially adjusted to my urban environment. (That's one of the things that makes me so efficient at the office.)

At home (away from the office), I tell my wife the bad news: we've got to go to Europe—or somewhere. We brace ourselves with drinks. I take down the 24th volume of the *Encyclopaedia Britannica,* the one marked "Atlas and Index." We look at a map of Europe. Every place appears the same— not the same as every other place, but the same as every place looked last year—very abstract, very.

France is green. Spain is a sort of bluish-gray. Portugal is yellow. Italy is yellow, like Portugal. Ireland is green, like France. Great Britain is pink, like Switzerland. Iceland is yellow, more yellow, seemingly, than Portugal or Italy, surrounded as it (Iceland) is, by the blueness of the Atlantic. Iceland is a cool scene. The only place that approaches it is Sweden. Sweden is not completely surrounded by water, but almost. It wears the Baltic Sea like a stole. . .

Iceland is tempting. Odd thing: there is no *Baedeker* for Iceland—and no *Guide Michelin.* We look everywhere, on every shelf, above, below, and around the gap left by that 24th volume of the encyclopaedia.

All this is a charade. We know exactly where we're going. After New York, we like Spain best, blue-gray Spain. That's where we spent our last vacation. There we found our prison-away-from-prison: a country of strong schizoid (humanoid) contrasts: a country like New York is a city. . .

The canapes are served, and the world divides into those who continue to take that blue-gray cheese-spread they love, and the others, who keep looking, hoping that perhaps the green, perhaps the yellow. . . .

The world divides. . . . The wife of a retired business as-
sociate once wailed, "We went on a round-the-world cruise
last year, so we don't know where to go this year." There are
voices everywhere, some louder than others. . . . Perhaps this
lady remembers too much. Perhaps she remembers a bad
time, a time less comfortable than at home. . . . But then she
should whisper.

And what, really, do I remember of our last trip? It, too,
was a tourist experience compared with the day-to-day reality
of the blue fluorescent light, the crisp conditioned air, the
clicking of business machines, the muffled roar of the flusho-
meter in the executive john. . . . These, these are more real
than the sky, the air, the trees, the wine in Spain; more real,
too, than castanets and guitars. . . . All I can do—now, over
martinis—is pray silently for a safe return.

his: #3

There are the short trips too, weekends which lean heavily on sporty props: skis, skates, boats, beachballs, airmattresses, surfboards, guns, tennis racquets, golfclubs. . . . In any season on a Friday afternoon we can stand on the corner and watch the cars, heavy with equipment, crawl towards a tunnel or a bridge.

Or sometimes we are in one of them, a sports model befitting our activity, and we crawl along with the rest. Like children, we crawl towards some land or sea of play.

In Europe the cathedrals and museums are an excuse for shopping. Here the weekend games are an excuse for drinking. The props change—and the costumes—but the alcohol is constant; every place is a place to drink.

It takes a full weekend to unwind, to get into the spirit of play—and death, what the newspapers call "the weekend toll": a product not only of cars, but sun, campfires, backswings, rough seas, thin ice. . . the entire uncontrolled non-office environment.

Yes, by then, after a weekend, the stomach and nerves have unwound, gone slack in alcohol, and we are ready again to face the highways.

his: #4

A dream: my wife and I are driving in the country, find a house, buy it. It is large—maybe fifty or sixty rooms: enough for each of my wife's moods and mine, and those of our children.

We spend months (seconds, I suppose, in retrospect) decorating the place, deciding what stays, what goes, what is needed. During these months—no, *seasons*, I remember now; at least a full year—our energy, our fantasy goes, room by room, into fixing up this house. (Is it possible all that time, all that space was so briefly in my mind? And all those *things?* The wicker porch furniture? The billiard table? The moosehead mounted over the stone fireplace? The cast-iron bathtubs and sinks, blue with age? The silver lighthouse-shaped cocktail shaker which we polished? The mildewed books? Everything, everything in my head?)

Getting the place ready becomes a second life as real as that at the office, which I leave earlier and earlier on Fridays and return to later and later on Mondays. An associate refers to my "three-day week," not understanding that my week has become *seven* days.

My wife and I spend our vacation working on the house. There, as at the office, I feel I am doing something, making something, something real that I can share with my family, friends, and customers.

After that year or so (or that night or so or that moment

or so), the contractor calls to say his work is finished: the wicker furniture is painted white; the old tubs and sinks have been replaced by new ones; the moosehead is down, the shaped canvas is up; everything is perfect.

I can't wait. Though it is only Wednesday, I have my secretary cancel appointments for the rest of the week. (She has that power, that efficiency to give me time. . . distance. . . she, too, is a dream.)

My wife and I get into the car again and drive and drive, looking for that country road we saw first so long ago (it seems)—and since, so many times, through all those seasons. (Seasons, you see, exist in dreams.)

We cannot find the house, cannot find it during the day, nor at night with lights up bright. I am still driving—anxiously, desperately, smoking one cigarette after another—when I awake.

The room is dark except for shafts of dim streetlight coming through the blinds, making shadows that look like moose antlers. I strike a match—partly to make sure, partly because in the car I was, anyway, about to smoke another cigarette.

The antlers are not real. But neither is the room, the bed, my wife sleeping in it beside me. . . It is almost four (if the clock is real). . . . It will be five hours or so until I can return to a more certain reality.

his: #5

Property accumulates. The world seems filled with bar-
gains. Some ports are even called *free*. My wife always re-
turns from vacation with an extra suitcase. It contains small
tangible memories: leather and gold and silver and precious
stones, all worked by craftsmen of the Old World; musky
perfumes; the pelts of tiny elusive animals. . . . And I, for my
part, have arranged to have the larger memories (including
bottles of liquor) crated and shipped home: new paintings, old
icons, pottery. . . things that belong here. If we don't buy them,
who will?

Yes, property accumulates. Things pile quietly on
shelves and in closets; hang, hardly less quietly, on walls.
(There's a shriek at first as picture hook is driven into plaster,
but the sound dies—sometimes in seconds, sometimes in hours,
sometimes in days or weeks or years—but always the sound
dies and the object disappears, fades into the asymmetrical
background we've been taught to construct and worship since
the 'twenties. Invisibility was more difficult once, against a
symmetrical background; then people noticed when things
were out of balance.)

We do what others do to protect property. We have
learned to lock the doors (and, in learning, have sometimes
locked ourselves out). We have bought a dog, trained him,
watched him age and die, so confined here in the city that
we do not want to replace him. Whether we're here or not, we

keep a light on in the library (visible from the street, you will recall). Unlike dogs, bulbs are replaceable and (as their price goes up) we're told they are being made to have a longer life. Bulbs must be another one of those businesses to be in. It's so human the way they burn themselves out. So human, but not canine.

Oh yes, we carry insurance too, just like you. Each year the floater grows larger; the schedule of jewelry, furs, and fine art lengthens; the premium mounts. In the dialogue between people and property, property makes equal demands. Property must be fed daily, nourished, taken care of—like a dog or a child. Yes, we carry insurance. We're insured against fire, flood, theft—against everything except the property itself.

The robbers came. Until then we had thought robberies were something that happened to other people, victims. It had not occurred to us that we too might be part of a minority. And now, long since, I wonder if we are. What *was* that song, so faint now in the air? *It Takes Two to Tango. . .*

. . . *slow-slow-slow-slow fast-fast-fast-fast-slow. . .* My mind glides across the floor. . . whirls. . . dips. . . back to the early morning we discovered the theft, the systematic derangement of our possessions. . .

Thieves are discriminating. They want those things with the least identity: interchangeable things, things women love. They don't want art. Or a child. Or a dog (if we still had one). So, although *our* house was robbed, *my wife* was violated—she lost her furs and jewels.

I heard her say all the familiar things other people are supposed to say—and, indeed, have said—e.g., "We'd better have the locks changed and have bars put in the bathroom skylights." I watched her flip through the Yellow Pages and find

what she wanted under BURGLAR ALARM SYSTEMS. And
at the end of that day, tired from having dealt with insurance
agent and local precinct, but thankful that no one had been
hurt and that nothing irreplaceable had been lost, I suggested
one of those good restaurants we go to. Then my wife's voice
sounded more strange than ever. It was someone else's voice,
a public voice. She said quite loudly, "I have nothing to
wear." Fur, I suppose she meant, bleating like a sheared sheep.

hers: #1

This page could be blank. I'm placing it here only as a reminder. Later I'll claim equal time. Later you'll hear from me. But meanwhile I'll let him rave on and on, while I prepare a shopping list.

Are women supposed to talk more than men?

his: #6

I live in a world of designations. When the alarm goes off, five mornings a week, it shouts 7:30, always 7:30, always that same slim slice of pie held by those same two hands. For a moment I cling to that other world where there is no time and nothing is labeled, not even day or night. Beside me my mate sleeps on, Everywoman just a few minutes ago, a name now that I'm awake, but truly "my better half"—she is asleep.

I begin reading: the color of my urine—dark (what is it this time? scotch? beer? brandy? all three? more?); the yellow morning toothbrush (the night one is blue, but some days —some days I'm confused); the pressurized toothpaste, the smaller can, the one that's red and white (I'm not really reading yet, just shapes and colors—I might be asleep, were it not for that gray thing in the mirror); the larger can now, the one that's blue and white (I shake it, knowing the directions by heart, as they say; and the gray thing turns lathery white, then pink, then gray again: a compromise, the way my teeth turn pink when I brush them, then yellow when I rinse). Another boozy pimple to squeeze from my boozy nose (a bit past pink, tending toward purple), and I step into my dressing room.

Is it possible I'm not awake? Everything's so beautiful. It's a New York day. I feel it out there, beyond the gray window. Once again the morning sun has hit the thermometer, but I'm not misled. I know. I know not to read numbers. I know to look at the people in the street, the eager ones who have been up for hours studying the weather map or taking deep breaths before their open windows—they're wearing the right clothes; it's cool. I get into my briefs, thankful that the waist stretches. 36—the size is prominent inside the elastic band designed to hold up the elastic pouch which my doctor said will give me just the mild support I need. (That was at the same annual examination he recommended tranquilizers. He's an odd sort of doctor, an old-fashioned Freud-oriented internist who, like me, trusts the thermometer, but not completely.)

There's no need to read my suit labels (they're all the same, that of one of the best tailors in the East Fifties). From among twenty suits, all dark, ranging from gray, through midnight blue, to black, I choose a gray one. No chance to express myself here—or with socks or shoes or shirt—it is all like shaving: I want the world to trust me. Only with my tie (another narrow wedge, like 7:30) can I suggest a fragment of a dream. I select a green and blue striped foulard: bands of grass and sky, twisting 'round my neck, reversing as I make a knot (a little of each showing there) and now sky and grass, sky and grass. . . to just above my 36+ waist.

Breakfast is when I really begin to read: the *Times* with orange juice; advertising copy on cereal box for relief (in one portion, I'm told, I get ten times the amount of vitamin B1 I need); mail (delivered usually just as I finish). It drops with a thud outside the door, and I rush for it as though I were in my teens when letters came from friends and lovers. Now it is all impersonal demands: bills, solicitations, announcements, propaganda. . . and the magazines, like the newspapers, telling me what I should do, the books I should read, the plays and exhibitions I should see, the concerts I should hear, the sporting events, the TV programs, the lectures, the movies, the happenings. . . I drown in words, knowing the title (and the review) but not the work, knowing the verdict but not the case, knowing the score but not the game, knowing the reputation but not the person, knowing the name but not the object. . . knowing nothing. My mind is a blank catalogue, indexed but full of empty cards. I cheer myself remembering that even the inscriptions on gravestones disappear.

. . . packaging, masks, facades, aliases, false signatures. . . Was there *his* John Hancock once as well as *ours*? Did men write their own books and speeches? Could one tell the players without their numbers? The buildings?

Now one bank is more openly inviting than the next. There's glass everywhere and signs that might say ENTER or PUBLIC PROPERTY or FRIENDLY DOG. . . . Aloof manners have died along with thick stone walls. . . . We're all not-reading the same things. We're all not-seeing the same things. We're all not-hearing the same things. But we're reading, seein, hearing the same things *about* them.

I get up from breakfast with my brain mushed out (words and cereal in the crevices), prepared for work, for the real words and the real numbers in the real letters and the real contracts and the real statements. Work, like death, is real—perhaps they end in a tie.

As I walk to the office I wonder if anyone will recognize the dream looped so carefully around my neck.

his: #7

I hear the cry of artists (painters mostly) for help, for love, for recognition—in short, for that abstraction of all these: money. It is so easy for me at my desk to buzz and have my secretary type a check. An electric machine does her work. A signature does mine. Or does the artist do both of ours? Or do we do the artist's? It is confusing to follow the complex flow of energy—money is that abstract.

But sometimes as I face a check there *is* effort. I don't want to be patron or philistine: the choice: to sign or not. (The blank, the negative response is as analyzable, under an artist's sensitive gaze, as a signature. Both lack character. For another $5, or 50, or 500 a fuller, more detailed reading can be had.)

I think of Samuel Johnson biting Lord Chesterfield's cool hand: "Is not a Patron, my Lord, one who looks with unconcern on a man struggling for life in the water, and, when he has reached ground, encumbers him with help?" Yes, since then (Feb. 7, 1775), to be a patron, to be fatherly is to be a philistine. Definitions are elastic; they stretch beyond individuals to include institutions. Foundations, universities, corporations are our patrons now. What man is strong enough to be a patron?

I lean back in my leather chair, juggling the two choices and looking at the acoustic ceiling for alternatives there among the simulated travertine veins. I negotiate with myself, considering various amounts, and then (as though it had never before occurred to me) various deserving payees, deciding finally on *me*. Why not, I wonder, give my money away all at once to me, form some great self-nourishing foundation?

A revelation: it is more blessed to receive than to give. To give has become humiliating. I would like to share the pride with which others receive fellowships, grants, endowments, benefactions, subsidies. . .

The ceiling offers no help. If I did not grip the chair, and if it did not grip me (in perfect posture), I would be sucked up there in among those veins which lead to sound-vaults where everything is stored, wrapped in synthetic silence, screams as well as whispers which will not escape until the building is torn down.

Listen sometime to the words behind the screech of crowbars and the tattoo of the wreckers' hammers. Listen also to the screech, the tattoo behind words. These sounds we make should not be treated lightly. They should not come and go so easily. They should be carved in stone or cast in bronze, MADE PERMANENT WITH EFFORT.

But I digress—I had been thinking about signing my name on a check. I had been trying to get at the meaning of that gesture, that single small expenditure of energy which would draw upon other energy, past energy, stored in another vault, just as the artist's image (more energy) is stored in paint.

But he has signed his painting. And I will sign my check. We will swap energy. And I will try not to think about who is patronizing whom.

his: #8

It impresses them at the office, how few words I use—mostly numbers. My letters and memoranda are brief and to the point, the decimal point. I round off cents to the nearest dollar, dollars to the nearest thousand, with the same efficiency as I clear my desk and avoid taking work home (except in my head).

Lawyers expand on my style. They have one of their own; they carry those briefcases—anything but brief—full of words. They repeat my numbers and spell them out in parentheses, and they create galaxies of synonyms around each verb. For me there is *one* verb: WORK. I can see it now in a contract: *The party of the first part shall work, labor, toil until . . .* until the synonyms run out, until at last another seemingly specific date occupies what's now a general blank. When it comes to blanks, lawyers are no different than anyone else. They know the need to fill them, whether with dates or prices or names or (ultimately) lives. No primitive artist faces his *horror vacui* with more concern. The lawyer in his office, like the caveman in his cave, knows that an empty space is essentially a stretch of time . . . words are time . . .

You will think perhaps that because I conserve words—not only their number, but their volume—I am less generous than lawyers, women, or others. A reasonable conclusion, that—the negative one of my wife, as well as the positive one of my co-workers—and yet, and yet . . . back in that empty

space, reading between the lines, listening to silence, I hear
what may seem a monologue to you (a whispered one at that)
as the screaming search for another voice, a response, a dia-
logue . . . It's deafening, the roar of all the words out there in
all their different disguises of language, accent, style, argot . . .
whispering, saying, shouting, singing, "Where are you? Where
Are You? WHERE ARE YOU?"

An opera, an opera without audience, maybe a re-
hearsal—opera nevertheless, neither heavy nor light, neither
grand nor bouffe, but *work*. Phrases from Wagner mingle with
those from Gilbert & Sullivan and The Beatles; in the back-
ground there's the sound of bombs and flowers opening their
lips. . . .

Are journalists more generous than poets? Are con-
sumers more generous than manufacturers? (These are the
questions I ask as I sit in my office, dictating the essence of con-
tracts, dealing with customers, playing my cards. . .) Are they
loaded questions? Is "Where are you?" Is "Where am I?"

Words, words, words . . . the grit and the oil in the eco-
nomic machine, a paradigm of life. . . . Do we write words to
preserve them (for possible future use) or to get them out of
the way (so the present can exist)? Are we preserving silence
or dissipating sound?

How quietly Mallarmé's dice fall on the page.

How quickly Rimbaud's vowels turn black and white.

Loaded questions are loaded sighs.

I return home from my secretary to my wife. I fix a drink,
open the evening paper. Her mouth opens with it: a condi-
tioned reflex. She cannot bear to see me read. Something
about my being involved with other people's words makes her
want to talk. There's that day's mail, telephone calls, shop-

ping. There's a joke a neighbor told. There's something cute one of the children said. Or—a carry-over from grade school—there's something that starts as a question and ends as a speech:

"How can you drink while you read? For me drinking is a social pleasure. When I drink. . . ."

I put down the paper and she picks it up. Not only does she like to talk when I read, but when she reads.

"Did you see the item about. . . .?"

"Yes."

But sometimes, "No." Then she is triumphant. She glows with having given me something in exchange for what she supposes must be my long hard days at the office, a subject which I don't discuss and she's not permitted to, a forbidden subject, taboo.

Dinner is almost silent, conversation having been exhausted. But afterwards there may be a play or movie or concert (she insists she cannot enjoy these alone) or, if we're in, another publication—in any case, a multitude of possibilities for talk. . . . Perhaps we are in, and I go back to the item I missed in the paper (to get it just right, numbers and everything), or I move on to *Fortune* or *Business Week*: my style books, my commonplace books; but, for my wife, child's play, hardly worth her casual interruptions. She waits for bigger game, a real challenge. Proust, Joyce, Svevo, Stevens . . . these, these, in my hand, are what truly inspire her to talk; these she finds harder to distract me from than newspapers and magazines.

So the evening goes, another compounding of monologues, authors' voices in relation to those of their characters in relation to mine in relation to my wife's; another opera (*pas un autre opéra, mais un opéra autre*), *something else.*

There's just one other time when my wife likes to talk as

much as when I'm reading: that's when we're making love.
Then her memory works. She remembers more letters (a bill,
an invitation), more telephone calls, people she met on the
street, recipes . . .

I am silent, except to the extent I cause the squeaking of
the bed.

"Say something nice."

"What d'you want me to say?"

"*You know.*"

"I'm saying it."

"Say it with words."

I say it and wonder if my reading in bed would improve
the dialogue.

Later (i.e., after):

"I don't understand how a man can be as cold as you are,
as silent, as stony—and yet as passionate. . . . D'you know what
I like best? The surprises. Waiting. Not knowing what you'll
do next."

"Perhaps I'd like some surprises too."

"No. Men know what they want, go after it, get it. You
have that. Women have surprises. They're ours. You mustn't
ask for them."

Still later, I try my hand (my wife's typewriter) at con-
crete poetry:

Exercise pad

I love you.
I love you.
I love you.
I love you.
I love you.

I love you.
I love you.
I love you.
I love you.
I love you.
    Love,
Even in my mind and on the typewriter, it's exhausting
to say over and over again. I have barely enough energy left
to sign my name.

Well, that—that concrete poem, with its rhythm as con-
stant as that of a pneumatic drill—*that*, signed, goes to my
wife. This goes to my journal:

My exercise pad is my bed.

Journal entries are only that, entries: the keys to locks
which protect other locks, in a world that should be open any-
way, which is what keeping a journal is all about: solitary
fucking: masturbation: ejaculation.

his: #9

All my systems are shot: electrical, plumbing, heating, air-conditioning—nothing works. Everything is rusted and creaking. Fluids are polluted. Ideas and emotions get lost within me. There is no clear passage.

I take my temperature often, as the doctor said I should. Sometimes I am overheated. Sometimes I am cold. The thermostat, if it exists, if it too has not disintegrated, is no longer set at 98.6. 98.6 is an accident now, not a habit. The mercury dances above and below the line, plays in waves of unpredictable saliva. That mercury in its narrow glass prison—and me in mine. That mercury, so volatile in my mouth—and the other, inert, amalgamated with silver in child-hood fillings, done before I was promoted to gold. Those first fillings talk to the later ones, the gold inlays. I feel the electric messages go back and forth, past bridgework and plate. Like me, my teeth talk in whispers. They speak of what they've known: good food and bad, both going down and coming up; fermentations; distillations; the smoke of tobacco and more exotic plants; human flesh; hair. . . the things one can get his teeth into. Yes, these teeth, what's left of them, memories mostly, once had a grip on life and now rock loosely in their gums, whispering of the past.

Did I say the saliva was unpredictable? I was speaking of its temperature. Its color is predictable—always pink, a bloody pink—as predictable, I was about to say, as if the doctor had prescribed a rectal thermometer. But I can't say that either. I watch my stool—doctor's orders, again—and it varies from a yellow as pale as straw to a brown that's almost black: a Spanish palette. However, I have no time for esthetic digressions—I have so little time—and you are wondering, anyway, why the doctor prescribed using an oral thermometer. Perhaps you know the anus is more accurate than the oris. Well, that is the truth, one of the few truths I am left with after all these years. It is a corollary of the even more basic truth that the body—the body proper, not the mouth—doesn't lie. Except in bed, I should qualify.

The doctor was considerate. I must make my rather unseemly confession more specific: I have piles. There, at the very core of what's left of my body, I am most vulnerable, most tender, most pained. There, again, is the bloody pink, in with that palette of Spanish earth-colors. . . . I don't know why at first I hesitated to mention this. I don't know why, once having decided, I adopted a confessional tone. It's nothing really, just part of my life. Perhaps piles acquire a disproportionate significance when they belong to you—everything does. Especially pain.

I am hooked. How fashionable that sounds. How mid-century. . . . I can see you seeing the marks, the tracks on my arms. Even if they aren't there. That my addiction is evidenced only by these other marks I make on paper must be disappointing. As disappointing as an endless story. But that *is* my addiction: to talk forever to these empty sheets of paper, passive (theoretically) as women, never answering back, never permitting the dialogue I once dreamed of. To talk (even in whispers), to make these marks in air and on paper, and never never to receive any words but my own. It is a lonely business, though my choice. Like yours, an exercise in control. The drug one chooses makes so little difference. Stone. Paint. Words. Business. Medicine. Law. Science. Politics. . . .

The world is yours. Yours and mine. It's a shame we can't share it. I listen carefuly as I write, wanting to hear your voice. Are you whispering?. . . There's a dog barking in the garden—and somewhere the hum of air-conditioning and cars. Controlled temperature. Controlled movement. Controlled everything but me. Now control exists only out there. I read about other worlds, responding at least as much as this paper does to the pressure of my pen. I know there are those who bowl 300 and those who pitch hitless runless games and those who write sonnet sequences and those who think in light years and those who plunge scalpels (or needles) into brains . . . . . and those . . . and those . . . I accept their existence but know none of them and none knows me. . . . We can't discuss the strength of the opposing team, the size of the field, the mood of the audience, anything; because the game is always solitaire (patience, some call it).

Masturbation is solitaire. Love is masturbation without guilt (i.e., with an accomplice). . . I hate words when they sound like this—cool as the twentieth century and tired as the eighteenth—but what am I to do? I take dictation. The rest is up to you. You can rearrange the words. They're no longer mine. *Imagine* a sense of property about words—even about their arrangement. NO.

Control! I laugh, having believed in it once, having envied it later, and even more now, when none of the valves work. Control, another fantasy that eventually disappears.

I have done my time, paid my dues. You can learn nothing from me as I am. But as I was . . . as I was . . . I will try to recall:

The desire, the lust—they're what's gone. Everything excited me then: the countryside covered with green pubic hair, blue breasts floating in the sky, red lips everywhere. A woman could not walk down the street who was safe from my fantasies, my once shimmering palette. Then I thought about women all the time. And now they don't exist. Then, if buildings were phallic, streets were vaginal. Then . . .

And now there's the click of high heels on pavement, but not the click of hips. The countryside (a pun) is gone, the grass (another pun?) is gone, the sky is gone—all gone so quietly. Shhh . . . old age is about remembering what once we wanted . . .

As I shrink the world shrinks. It is not only the women in the street who gradually disappear, but friends who through the years have become acquaintances and relatives who have become less than acquaintances, strangers without (for me) even the possibilities of strangers.

Parents, aunts, uncles, cousins, all are as far now from my immediate family as my immediate family is from the office. The circles surrounding me appear in an order quite the opposite from what Confucius described.

There was a time long ago when I saw what's now the outer ring of relatives at weddings. They told me then that some day I would get married. Now I see them at funerals. They don't have to tell me. I know.

wHISpers
wHispERS
wHISpers
wHispERS
wHISpers
wHispERS
wHISpers
wHispERS
wHISpers
wHispERS
wHISpers
wHispERS
wHISpers
wHispERS
wHISpers
wHispERS
wHISpers
wHispERS
wHISpers
wHispERS
wHISpers
wHispERS
wHISpers
wHispERS
wHISpers
wHispERS
wHISpers

Part Two
(the early 'sixties continued)

hers: #2

Now.

I have just read through the entire pile of papers my husband calls "whispers," nine of them so far, neatly typed by his secretary (I hate her, I hate her).

Him and his whispers, her and her perfect margins (with none for error)—I could scream.

Those whispers are lies, all of them. I don't mean he says things that aren't true, but he doesn't say so many things that are. Those silences he raves about, that empty space—lies, all lies. Omissions. . . . And he's not very old—or tired either, though he may be tired of disguising himself for business, like some member of Artists Anonymous (a little joke of his). Yes, that may be tiring. . . .

When we're *alone together*—what an ambiguous phrase! —there *is* communication; our thoughts mingle, breed, however quietly. . . . And when the silence is broken, that's all that's broken. Words destroy nothing else, any more than thoughts. It's actions that kill. And he acts nice.

But how could you know that, raveled as you are in his dreams of some lesser self, listening to that brusque sardonic joyless voice—how could you know? Is there even a hint of the physical man, moving through space, doing something? You would think he spent his life at his desk. Well, he may consider himself a sort of Hamlet-as-businessman, but I am no Ophelia, *no Ophelia*—it's hard to say. No anything is hard.

There was a time when I would gladly have surrendered my identity to his, dissolved myself in him. He made that impossible. He never told me who he was. I'm not sure *he* knows. If he does, he is a secret he is unwilling to share.

His business associates tell me he's good at his job (whatever he does, precisely—I don't know). Friends say he's brilliant at chess. Our children love him. I love him. How can such a man pretend he's alone? Why even when he reads—not the newspapers or financial publications, but less serious things: novels, poetry—when he reads these, his lips move; he must be speaking to *someone*. Me, I assume. . .

He's no more alone than I. At the office, at lunch, at conferences, eight hours a day or more, five days a week, he must be *surrounded*.

I'll make it stronger: I'm more alone than he. I have him, the telephone, the measured voices in cookbooks, casual relationships with shopkeepers and neighbors. . . . Perhaps when he leaves the office he wants to be alone. Perhaps in bed. . . .

That things must end is something he cannot accept—I suppose no man in business can. For me everything is endings: sex, dinner, shows, books, life itself. . . .

The myth is that women are unsatisfied, but it's men who always want more—not more from us, but from themselves. They dream of endless love, and their bodies can't support that dream. Ours can. If the world belongs to us, the dream at least belongs to them.

After sex, as I drift from him toward sleep, I hear him tossing, lighting cigarettes, talking (to himself, I wonder, or to me?).

"What? What'd you say, dear?"

"Nothing."

"Is there something on your mind, something bothering you?"

"Nothing. Go to sleep."

When he thinks I am asleep he turns on the lamp and reads, or opens that notebook he keeps on the night table and writes some cryptic phrase: *alone together* was really his, in that little book, where, I suppose, he thinks his whispers begin, if not on the empty page.

Beginnings—I accept them as I accept endings. For me things begin, before any phrase or empty page, with his silent playful tongue in my ear—or anywhere.

Beginnings—it is another day; he has gone to work; the children have gone to school. I drink coffee, straighten the bedroom, and look in his notebook as I do each morning. (Odd, he has no objection to that and yet won't let me ask about his days at the office.) There is a new entry:

Is there something on your mind?"

Insomnia means *thinking about death.*

It doesn't sound like him—like anyone after making love. I wonder what he was reading. There's a heavy book, almost a thousand pages, on top of the pile on his night table, *Sex Offenders: An Analysis of Types*—he reads everything, *everything*. A matchcover indicates his place in the introduction, and there a passage is marked:

If a man walking past an apartment stops to watch a woman undressing before the window, the man is arrested as a peeper. If a woman walking past an apartment stops to watch a man undressing before a window, the man is arrested as an exhibitionist.

I am amazed. See, my husband and I do have a sort of

telepathic bond. That paragraph relates exactly to what I was saying: *Is it a man's world or a woman's?* And yet I don't see the man as a victim, either. In this little legal parable I see the man, as always, receiving top billing. That's all—neither oppressor, nor oppressed—but placed, *on top.* You might say it's a biological law—God knows I avoid those couples where the woman's on top; freaks; against nature. . . . I whisper this to you. He won't let me say it out loud. It's another rule, like not asking about what happened at the office. He's against generalizations, simplifications, answers. I get around him sometimes by answering in the form of a question—or vice-versa. But he's not easy to get around. Usually he just looks up from the book and glares.

Those books, each one seemingly an indictment, each one saying, through him, *Read me.* But when would I have time? The days go, given to him, the children, meals, house . . . given willingly. . . . . Sometimes—maybe always, now—he looks so disappointed as he studies the cover of yet another cookbook I'm reading. Once, on the subject of dreams, he said, "Yours are in your stomach." It was hours later before I thought of saying, "At least I share my dreams with you."

Neither remark was fair. The first time I was pregnant he spent the winter reading Proust aloud to me. The second time, *The Spoils of Poynton,* a lesser effort. But always, always he recommends the things he likes, wants to share them, feels rejected when I read a cookbook instead. I wonder if *Sex Offenders* will be on his recommended list. 923 pages! God! At least cookbooks have a plot, an end.

He says there's always time for what we want to do, that one chooses, say, between Henry James and a soufflé. I admit the choice, and that admission is, I suppose, what really hurts him—he might prefer to think I don't know what I'm doing.

But I do know what he believes is lasting and what is transient—only for me these are a matter of degree. I may prefer what seems most transient, but, like every woman, I know that nothing lasts.

Cookbooks, fashion magazines, today's list of "specials" at our neighborhood Gristede's—these interest me, these are my classics. . . . He understands, I think. He has stopped suggesting that I get a full-time cook, spend less time with the children, use a caterer when we entertain. . . . He no longer tries to rob me of my life, and in a few more years—who knows?—perhaps he'll understand that he can't give me his.

I don't want it—that's the point.

Even though I don't know exactly what he does at the office, I know it must be useful—he's paid well, we live comfortably. But his reading? His marked passages? His cryptic notes? His so-called "whispers"? Why? For what? Some senseless battle against time? Against me? Against the children? All they know is: "Quiet, Daddy's working." Those rare weekend afternoons he spends with them mean so much more than anything he can ever write.

And the reading. . . Where does it get him? What has it done for him? Is he happier? The answers are *nowhere, nothing, no,* in that order. He says so himself: that the process is endless; that one book leads to another; that there are no answers, that, at best, one meets another person, hears another voice. . . .

I do *that* at cocktail parties. No, that's too flip, an echo of something I might have said years ago when I tried to meet him in his arena, before he made me understand I have my own. Then, in those early years, I felt inferior, not knowing what was going on in all those books, in all those other people's minds, in his. . . . He convinced me it was not a question of knowledge, but of pleasure. "The rest disappears," he said, "the memory fails—all that's left is having liked something— someone—or not. Knowledge is pleasure. Intelligence is happiness. You're smarter than I am." How I've hung onto those words, wondering sometimes if he meant them, or simply gave them to me as a gift, or if perhaps he was just saying, you're a woman and I'm a man.

He and his chess-playing friends and his business associates seem happy only when they're at their games. These men are just like me—it's the games that are different. There's something as mysterious and ambiguous about the words *stalemate* and *checkmate* as *alone together*: all tell stories of marriage. And yet, after hours of pushing pieces around a board, he throws the words away, having said, you remember, that words should be cast in bronze or carved in stone (in crisp Roman letters, I suppose, over a double-grave). If they were my words, I'd let them curve freely, beyond the grave, in flowing tubes of neon.

I like that high TIME/LIFE sign, flashing those big words, announcing (as we walk west) the world that lies beyond. Broadway and the Village are more real to me than Wall St. banks and Park Ave. office buildings, the changing words on marquees so much more real than the symbols on a teleregister. I understand when there's a Bogart revival; Syntex, as a growth stock, is more abstract.

I like life in the street—and just off the street. I like fat salty pretzels, hot dogs with everything, hamburgers as thin as a dime, jellied apples, orange drinks that are orange only in color (and a different splendid taste), chestnuts. . . I adore chestnuts. Their shells are the one thing I can throw on the street without feeling I'm a litterbug. Shells were meant to be thrown away; somehow they're not waste. . . . When other peo-

ple count sheep I invent exquisite minimal diets—the mar-
riage of a single food and a single beverage. Chestnuts and
orange drink is one such diet. I see myself growing golden and
slim on an island—Manhattan perhaps, before Peter Stuy-
vesant made that deal.

And just off the street: I like shops, restaurants, supermark-
ets. . . . I hardly walk on Park Ave. any more—I cross it. The
banks, the stock brokerage offices, the showrooms have ruined
it, turned it into a place where there's nothing to buy but
money. These buildings I'd tear down and on their plots plant
trees. The others—the ones on Broadway, on Fifth, on Madi-
son—I'd cut off at the second floor. . . .

I know: if it had depended on me the human race would
never have reached the 1960's. There'd be no trips to the
moon. Even the wheel wouldn't exist—as my husband has told
me. But I like to walk.

He reads articles—even writes them sometimes—on the
technological revolution, its implications, social, economic,
political. . . . He tells me about new ideas in drugs, computers,
packaging, communications, transportation. . . . He bought
Xerox in the low twenties, Texas Instruments when it was
issued. . . However, he has to have a very bad hangover to take
an aspirin, he's lost in a supermarket, anxious on planes,
bored by most TV. . . . And if a repairman says something
needs a new sealed unit, my husband shrugs (along with me).

"We have to play the game," he said once.

"What game?"

"The sealed unit game. My game. My life."

That was one of the few times he talked about his work.

hers: #3

I don't know where the morning goes. A few cups of black coffee. Phone calls. A glance at the *Times* (my parts, far past that gloomy front page). Phone calls. Shopping lists. Phone calls. The mail. Phone calls. . . .

I cradle the phone between my cheek and shoulder—he used to think only secretaries can do that—leaving my hands free for other things, doing several at once; and yet nothing gets done. Revolutions are made, things are discovered, records are set—and I don't hear about them 'til dinner, if then. The shopping lists are never complete; I'm always going back to some store or making another call. The mail gets scrambled with the list (often on the backs of letters). . . .

Is it the lack of executive ability or, as my husband thinks, the lack of a secretary?

"You're unprotected. Too many calls come through."

"I want them all. I never get too many."

"But you could have them when you want, at your convenience."

"And have a secretary talk to my friends?"

"Well, then a part-time girl, one or two days a week, just to check bills and pay them and take care of routine correspondence. . . You could read in the morning."

"I like reading my bills, thank you."

"A dictating machine then? I could take the cartridges to the office, have your things typed there." He pauses, his eyes light up like those bulbs in cartoons. "With a dictating ma-

chine and answering service you could have most of the ad-
vantages of a secretary, without any sense of intrusion or of
having to keep someone busy—"

"Please! You have your Miss Dictating Machine/Miss
Answering Service. Let me have my bills."

For a moment he looks at me as though I'm completely
irrational and disorganized. Then he opens a book and begins
to read.

"You understand, don't you?" There's no answer. "I ap-
preciate your wanting to help, but—" The rest is implicit. I
wait for a word from him, a nod, anything. But still no answer,
nothing, silence. "D'you know why *you* need a secretary? Be-
cause you're a lousy answering service—that's why." A smile,
a response at last. I think he understands. He has not brought
up the subject again.

Not directly. However, there are references now and then
to how well *she* does things at the office. He doesn't necessarily
mention her name—she's just there, by implication, as a stand-
ard of comparison. The phone rings. It's for him. I call him
when he's in the middle of a poem by Stevens. (*She* would
have taken a message.) I fill out a school application for our
son. It's just a little sloppy, so little that if it keeps him out
of this school I don't want him to go there. (*Her* paragraphs
are neat, *her* margins straight, *her* touch steady.) Well, these
are things she's paid for. It's the other things she does for him
that I resent: the loose buttons she fixes, the shopping she does,
the Christmas cards. . . .It's true, he asks me first, but I'm busy
and she has nothing else to do.

It's no wonder men marry their secretaries or have affairs
with them. The situation is so beautifully abstract, the hours
so regular, the call so pure (doing only what *he* wants). Yes,
these girls can be mothers, mistresses, servants, pen pals all

at once—everything but wives. Or, to put it another way, they *are* wives, abstracted from home, children, everything but bed. . . . All affairs, it occurs to me now, are affairs with secretaries. Affairs are, by definition, abstract. Men have them because they think they should. Women oblige. In marriage love-making isn't the basic game; in an affair it is.

"If we were on a desert island—"

"There are none left."

I understand if when he's here, at home, with me and the children—surrounded by confusion, distraction, detail—he dreams sometimes of other women. But when he's with them, I'm sure he dreams of me. I must believe that. Over and over I tell myself that—that, and that an affair more often indicates dissatisfaction with oneself than with one's mate.

I asked him about his dreams. He said, "I dream only of you, but you're always disguised as another woman."

Well, let them, the secretaries of the world, sew on buttons, address Christmas cards (for me Christmas is one day, for children; it doesn't begin in January and end in December)— let those secretaries do what they want, as long as they keep their hands off my husband. If on this subject I sound shrill, it's not because I'm jealous; it's just that I don't like a contest that's unfair.

"It's bad enough when you can't reach someone on the phone because there's no answer. Then he simply doesn't want to speak to you. But when you get a busy signal it clearly means he prefers to speak to someone else."

"You're nuts," my husband replies. "Crazy. Delightfully crazy."

I like the progression from *nuts* to *crazy* to *delightfully crazy*: I hope he's right.

hers: #4

Even now, so young, the children are beginning to move away. Their school days grow longer. They spend more time with friends. Last summer our son went to camp. This summer our daughter will go. Then prep school for him, college for both, marriage. . . I feel their absence, a sort of growing pain (their growth, my pain), a growing vacuum, stretching out through the years. . . . I feel their absence—and anticipate it—as my husband does their presence.

How can he complain? He sees so little of them really: at breakfast; an hour or so before dinner; some small part of the weekend. I see them the rest of the time, *want* to anyhow, and yet they are moving away. He says that's our job, to prepare them to leave. But who, I ask, is going to prepare me?

I was prepared once, soon after they were born, during those early years of interrupted sleep, crying demands, the shock of lost freedom. . . (Is any child ever born at a convenient hour? Does any child cry at a convenient hour?) However, being needed becomes a habit. I need them now to need me.

I had thought the gain and the loss would balance out. I had thought that what one lost and what one gained were about the same—or, if you were lucky, that the gain was greater than the loss. The point is freedom and parental satisfaction—call them that if, again, you're lucky—are different things; they can't be equated. It's like at school when they tell you you can't add apples and pears. But now I wonder if even two apples

are ever the same. I wonder if, in life and not on some black-
board, an eye for an eye or a tooth for a tooth exists. Isn't it
mostly an eye for a tooth and a tooth for an eye?

I ask questions as my children do (did):

"Whatever you do to have a baby, if you want another
baby, do you have to do it again?"

"Do angels make b.m.'s?"

"Where was I when you were a little girl?"

"Will I ever be a child again?"

"Does everyone die sometime? I don't want to—not even
once." (My son's voice is so much like my husband's.)

"Are you staying home tonight?"

"No," I reply.

"You went out last night, and two wrongs don't make a
right."

Questions moving towards assertions, you see. . . . When
our daughter was born, our son said:

"We were all so happy together when there was just me."

He had something there. Now the little one flirts with my
husband. (We have a potential secretary in our nest.) She
opens a pack of cigarettes for him—all wrong, but so intently
performing a service, an act of love—and he says:

"I love you more than any other little girl in the world."

"Then what do you want to do?"

"Go on loving you."

"Go on."

"What?"

"Kiss me. Hug me."

He does.

"Your face is rough."

"I didn't shave today."

"Then kiss me like this." She puckers her mouth and

kisses him on the lips. "This way it doesn't hurt."

And:

"I want to grow up as big as you are."

"That's very tall for a girl. Why do you want to be that tall?"

"So when Mommy dies we can dance."

And. . . And. . . And. . .

Enough of children's fantasies about their parents. What about parents' fantasies? There was a newspaper story about a mother who threw her four-year-old daughter in front of a subway train. The mother told the police she wanted her girl to become an angel.

hers: #5

"But what do you really do?" my friends ask, gesticulating with long arty fingers covered with paint or plaster. Others stand by sternly, with hands at their sides, weighed down by piles of sheet music or text books on social psychology. They wait for an answer.

And the answer is easy, easier than when they ask me what *he* does. "I have my husband, my children, my home—"

"But statistically—"

"—your husband will die before you."

"—your children will grow up and leave."

"—your house will be empty."

"—surely you see the risks?"

They sound like stockbrokers telling me to diversify. I marvel at the security they find in their arts and sciences. Yes, I go to their group shows and recitals, hear their lectures, glance at their articles (some published, some not). Yes, I acknowledge their graduate degrees. And yet, as their careers assert themselves (not only in person, but in the morning mail, on the telephone), demanding always that their accomplishments be recognized, they, too, will have to accept my identity—sex: female; occupation: housewife.

Even my mother-in-law is painting now, and my mother is giving a course in remedial reading. I am all alone, a rebel.

I like that thought: I tell my husband.

"You're an artist," he replies, "all housewives are artists."

hers: #6

Ten for dinner tonight—that's why I'm doing my hair: I like it to look really dark and brilliant when we entertain. I do it—rubber gloves, rinse, plastic cap, after-rinse—when my husband's at the office; he doesn't approve. I don't mean there's any issue about naturalness. After all, I'm not *changing* the color of my hair, but only bringing it back to what it was, washing away the gray as they say, rinsing not dyeing. No, he's not the sort who prefers gray to black, though it wouldn't be surprising if he did; what he objects to, once again, is the time—I could be doing something else. Reading maybe. Well, I don't just sit—it's not like when I had my teeth capped —I'm on the phone, I'm busy. His argument was hard to follow. It had something to do with the mustache he grew years ago. He said he shaved it off because it took too much time shaving with it on—and I had always thought he shaved it off for me. I rinse my hair for him.

Ten is such a perfect number for dinner, better than eight or twelve—I can sit at one end of the table, flanked by men; my husband at the other, flanked by women; and still, right down the sides, the boy/girl rhythm is maintained, we have our Noah's Ark . . . . Separated by four couples, I feel as close to him as when we eat alone—perhaps because he talks more, even if I can't hear what he says.

The flowers, the candles, the table linen, the food itself, me myself— these are what I want him and our guests to talk

about. I want them to acknowledge that everything didn't just
happen. My husband and I have talked already, before drinks,
before the first guest arrived. He said the table looked beauti-
ful and I looked beautiful.

"But don't you think my pink pajamas would be better?"

"No, that's fine."

He makes himself a drink and reads while I change. I was
right: the pink is better—maybe not perfect, but better.

"How d'you like this?" I ask him fifteen minutes later.
He continues to read, pretending not to hear. "HOW D'YOU
LIKE—?"

"It's very nice. . . . I told you I liked the other."

"Maybe I'll change back."

He looks at his watch, his great ally at times like this
(just as at other times the children are mine). "No, the com-
pany will be here any minute."

I have just selected a pair of brocade pants and my favo-
rite Pucci blouse, when the doorbell rings. I rush to get ready,
knowing even now that when finally I make my entrance he
will greet me with a complicated frown, a look intended to
say at least: 1) *You had all day.* 2) *I told you your first out-
fit looked fine.* 3) *You didn't have to ask my opinion but, since
you did, you should have accepted it.* Those will be some of
the arguments on his side. On mine there's this: I do now look
beautiful. In my head it's that simple. In actual dialogue,
years of it before we reached such shortcuts as his frown, it
would have ended about like this: *You can look beautiful
AND be ready on time.* Men want too much, always more.

The doorbell is ringing again. I rush from the bedroom
and receive this couple. I rush from the door and receive his
frown. He follows it with a martini: salve: just the way I like
it, very dry, on the rocks, with a twist of lemon peel, in a wine

glass (old fashioned glasses are for men; women were meant to hold a stem).

After three martinis (one couple is late), there are no longer any frowns in the world. Mouths smile, devouring his drinks and my hors d'oeuvres. Our roles are complementary. At table, too, I watch everyone's plates and he sees to the wine. And after dinner the brandy's his job, the coffee's mine. We have a fire going (his job again) and the smiles have turned to laughter.

It is a beautiful night. No one has even broken a glass. No one has argued. No one has done anything to spoil the evening—*my* evening. It *is* mine. I made it—with an assist from him.

It's almost three when the last guest leaves. I begin emptying ashtrays, clearing glasses. . . I know that any minute he will yell. "Can't that wait? She'll do it in the morning."

He does.

"She! Typical! I can't leave a mess like this for Ruby. Maybe to you she's just a number on social security and withholding forms. Ruby and I have a *relationship*."

"Yes. She works for you. You pay her to clean. That's the relationship."

"I'll only be a few minutes. If you helped I'd be done twice as fast."

"Five times. But I have to be at the office at nine. You can sleep."

"I couldn't. Not knowing that Ruby would walk in on this mess."

Within half an hour I finish putting things away. I tiptoe to the bedroom. He is still awake—silent, insomnious, annoyed—waiting for me. I go to the bathroom and insert my diaphragm. He needs me to put him to sleep.

hers: #7

It is another morning, after another party—this time at someone else's house. I thought my husband had gone to sleep when finally, after much morbid talk and brief sex, I did. But no, he must have stayed up writing. I found this:

Reunion

Even if I knew you were not listening / I would go on talking, just as if / knowing this would never be published / I wrote it all the same.

The lights are out. I write / with black ink on the night sky.

You see, my darling, I must / talk about death tonight. / tell jokes about it, defend myself. / You do see? I know / how you feel after all those drinks / and all that dancing (with others): / sleepy. And yet against / your desire there's mine.

I stroke your body wanting / to keep it awake. I call your pores / to attention. / I dive in / one ear and out the other. / In transit I reach for your heart.

"Even if love doesn't last / as long as death, / it is ours; death belongs to them." / Ha, a whispered secret. You stir, / forcing death out of your mind, / remembering living partners from earlier / this very night in some corner / of some living room. You re-create / an environment. You populate it. / Even I am there: the quietly jealous husband / before you became the tired wife. / God, how that party crowds our bed.

And other parties. And other partners. / *"Did you really dance the limbo once on broken glass?"*

Death comes up again / *as if by accident.* / *"How many of our friends have died?"* / *We count them like sheep.* / *All talked of suicide but . . .* / *but died in cars* / *as we may* / *die in bed.*

The conversation moves from who's / *dying with whom to who's sleeping with whom:* / *we talk about ourselves:* / *our words are ghosts* / *of people, things, ourselves again.*

$18,000,000 @ 7½%

The title made me think of a college reunion. He does have one coming up, but I doubt if he'll go—the distant past means so little to him. Yes, what he wrote is what I should have expected: the immediate past: just last night. That is his way: to jot down things that have just happened or just been said—or figures (like that *$18,000,000 @ 7½%*) for some conference he has scheduled. Yes, his work and I and, to a lesser extent, the children are what he must write about. Yes, *our* reunions: day-to-day, not year-to-year; a private habit, not a public event. Yes, he is my fucking partner, and I am his. I like that phrase, *my fucking partner;* it's as ambiguous as his *alone together.* I will give it to him. I will write it at the bottom of the page (just below *$18,000,000 @ 7½%*) and watch him smile.

As to those fences between phrases of *Reunion.* I'm not sure what they mean. They hold his words as though they were the precious segments of a poem. The businessman-as-poet, that's a funny idea. But no funnier than the housewife-as-artist, what he called me not so long ago. We cling to each other's words.

Well, I have said I accept endings: *men* can have their infinitely expandable universe.

No doubt he will go on making notes—late at night and between conferences and on weekends and holidays—just as other men fish, just as I cook. We do what we must, and what we do often appears isolated. Yet it is impossible for me to think of these words, both his and mine, as anything but a collaboration, a marriage. I think I will urge him to publish *our* book, unless that would jeopardize his career. Businessmen don't trust authors. Perhaps he should leave business. Perhaps *we* should.

wHISpers
wHispERS
wHISpers
wHispERS
wHISpers
wHispERS
wHISpers
wHispERS
wHISpers
wHispERS
wHISpers
wHispERS
wHISpers
wHispERS
wHISpers
wHispERS
wHISpers
wHispERS
wHISpers
wHispERS
wHISpers
wHispERS
wHISpers
wHispERS
wHISpers

Part Three
(the late 'sixties and early 'seventies)

hers: #8

Our life has a different rhythm now, no longer punctuated by his business (whatever it was): a different rhythm, but the same melody. Now time moves more freely and is harder to measure. He no longer sets his clock. He no longer shaves in the morning. He rarely wears a suit or even a jacket. He is here for lunch. He is here *almost all the time.* Once his departures and returns defined a day. The children's do that now; and their schedule changes, grows with them, has no fixed shape. Business was a simple clock—it ran weekdays from nine to five. "Retirement," as the world calls it—he hates the word—runs twenty-four hours a day, every day.

I'm no surer now of what he does than I was then of what he did. Even without the alarm, he continues to get up early; but without it (that announcement of a new day) and without my stirring, he leaves our bed more silently. Sometimes during the business years he would kiss—or even fuck—me goodbye. Now I suppose he thinks goodbyes are pointless—he isn't going anywhere. Nowhere but downstairs to have breakfast with the children, just as he always did. I remember his telling me (during those business years) how small my face looked in the morning, how much he liked to see it open up. Now I am lucky if, when he returns from breakfast, I hear his step on the stair—there's a squeak near our third-floor landing. Then, only then, maybe once a week, I call his name and he opens the door, walks quickly across the room, lifts the blinds, shuts the windows, kisses me, says he must get to work. *Must*, whatever that means, some uncontrollable habit.

He must get to his office: his office which was his dressing room, next to his secretary's office which was my dressing room. It's true he was willing to add another floor to the house, but I thought that would be too expensive and too much mess. He suggested moving to a larger house or apartment, and I vetoed those suggestions too. Even the thought of moving frightened me, still does: the dishes, the lamps, the spice jars, the souvenirs from trips we used to take (another time I'll come to that), the everything, in all everything's fragility, Louis Comfort Tiffany included, the whole breakable world of glass and china . . . the logistics perhaps ultimately leading to ballistics. . . .

He assured me that with his pension cashed in (forced savings, plus interest), stock options exercised, investments enhanced "multi-miraculously" (he used some such peculiar hyphenation), all we've ever bought worth *more* (the house, the Tiffany lamps, the art, everything—we are *rich*. He made me promise that if we didn't add to the house, didn't move, he would never have to hear about his depriving me of anything. I suppose that includes my dressing room. Still, I miss it. My clothes are more crowded now in the bedroom closets, and in the bedroom itself the light is poor, hardly conducive to subtle color coordination. (The housewife is an artist.)

You understand already, but there's more: He's shopping now. His packages come in from the best men's shops (places he never went when he was in business) and even from boutiques, in *my* stores, charged to *my* accounts. I said he's here *almost all the time*. Most afternoons he shops. The packages arrive: ten and fifteen dollar ties, thirty dollar shirts, sweaters that approach "three figures," as he would say, but end up *as*

one figure, *on* one figure, *his*. These are accessories, the little
gifts for himself. He sends me these too, or their equivalent
(a trifle more expensive when he's feeling guilty): a bright
scarf, a darling handbag, an elegant piece of *art nouveau* jew-
elry. . . But never anything *too* expensive. It's his made-to-
order stuff that costs, those jackets and slacks (his new leisure-
hours uniform, after lunch) which keep coming, on sculp-
tured hangers, in fancy plastic bags with the name of the tailor
embossed in gold; those shoes, hand-made by one of the few
British bootmakers in New York, those elegantly carved shoe-
trees. . . . I get nervous now when the doorbell rings. I feel
guilty when the black delivery boy—*man*, I mean—hands me
that heavy hanger or package. But my husband has it all
worked out, some theory about luxuries trickling through the
economy, products of tailors, chefs, jewelers, interior decor-
ators . . . the dying occupations of men who work with their
hands and wits . . . on wool, leather, fresh food, precious
metals, stone, wood, all the disappearing natural materials. . .
these mastercraftsmen and their middlemen who need us to
support their apprentices, helpers, unskilled laborers who
work only with their backs, often black (like those of the de-
livery men). All of which fits into some still broader theory
of wealth as the defender (and consumer) of arts, crafts, even
nature itself . . . everything from manuscript to tooled bind-
ing, from painting to carved frame, from rider's tweed, twill,
and leather to pedigreed horse following thoroughbred dogs
through private property landscaped by God and modified by
money. . . . His book, if he ever gets it done, will be a shocker.
He describes it as "an aggressively unfashionable answer to
Veblen." So is his life, this defender of "the consumer soci-
ety." He'll spend an entire morning attacking a phrase such
as "the artificial stimulation of wants in a saturated economy."

His theory: that without this stimulation there'd be no de-saturation, that the economy would choke. "There's nothing any more 'artificial' about stimulating consumption than production," he says. "I prefer the least possible external management and regulation. That's one reason why I left business. I like to write because there's no external reason to do so. Internal reasons suffice. I don't need stimulation, artificial or otherwise—" he pauses, smiles—"though sometimes a martini makes my thoughts flow faster."

Do I sound too much like Boswell? Well, other wives have their careers. I have my husband. His words amuse me. I hope I've got them right. He hates to be misquoted.

"I can't have dresses or furs fitted for you," he said one night at one of our restaurants. "You must cooperate, you must spend more, you owe it to the economy."

To oblige him I had caviar as appetizer, lobster as main course.

"A shore dinner," he remarked, pleased, selecting a vintage wine.

"Can we afford all this?" I asked.

"I hope so, but even if we can't it's—"

"I know: *good for the economy.*"

He justifies each bite we eat, each sip we swallow. For him every morsel, every drop is a sensation which can be traced finally to the home of some grape-picker in Bordeaux or some fisherman in Maine or some dark dishwasher hidden in the bowels of this restaurant. For him even the $5 tip he gives the captain is not money—it's perhaps a pair of shoes for the man's child. For me, it's all money, mouthfuls of money. I gag on guilt. I cannot yet accept our living better now than when he *really* worked.

"But that's part of what my book's about, the *pleas-*

ures of working for a large corporation, the *compensations.* . . .
Being self-employed is harder, I'm the toughest boss I've ever
had."

He says these things, but I watch him work. Or, if that's
not quite accurate, at least know his routine: maybe four hours
a day, five at the most, in his office. Surely the shopping isn't
research.

"Nothing is wasted," he reminds me, "everything is sal-
vageable."

"What about a marriage, separated by a wall I'm not
supposed to penetrate during the morning hours? Is that sal-
vageable? Do I have to slip notes under your door, write your
whispers for you?" He smiles the smug smile of the man in
control of himself, *myself, my home* . . . the production, distri-
bution, and consumption of wealth. . . His smile, his silence,
his "whisper" all focus suddenly as some occupational disease.
"And you call yourself an economist!" I scream.

The wall grows thicker for me, thinner for him. I'm not
supposed to move when he's working. I'm not supposed to
raise my voice. Even Ruby walks now on tiptoe, and she be-
comes tense when he emerges for lunch. He has told me all
he wants is a sandwich, but the sandwich is never right. It's
too dry, or the bread is stale, or the meat is thin.

"Why don't you just order a sandwich from the delica-
tessen? Or must the book be finished before you feel that we
can afford that luxury, that I deserve it?"

Maybe—I really don't know what he's doing up there:
that strange mixture of smiles, silences, and whispers that he
calls economics. Maybe it would be different if his book were
published. Maybe that would inspire a great sandwich.

(Here is where I stopped, hoping he would find my message before his secretary did. I see I have never actually said that I wish sometimes he was back at business. But business was his garret, and the home was . . . is . . . should be *mine*.)

hers: #9

It gets worse, no longer having business as an excuse for what separates us. I'm not even sure that that wall will do—as an excuse. I've come to the conclusion he's crazy, and not "delightfully crazy" either—nor ambivalent, as once I might have described his state. Is he writing a book in response to Veblen or us? That's my question, clear as it can be. I feel his eyes through the wall. And his ears. He has piercing ears.

Us or them? I want an answer. I won't accept some orthodox Freudian stance, by which I mean silence. Even a whisper, as such, will be barely acceptable.

What does it mean? Does he really think he can write about money with the same passion most people reserve for sex? Does he think that those phrases he uses—gold flow, balance of payment, gross national product—are poetry, foreplay?

I'm going to put this in an envelope marked PERSONAL. I want an answer.

his: #10

How near I was to the very brink of business, that high edge off which I might have fallen and lost myself forever, lost myself in business itself, in all its efficient comfort and distraction, its corporate armor at once protective and ornamental and cool. . . . I stood trembling on the lip of the valve at the heart of business, knowing that if I fell I would be crushed, incorporated by the corporation, institutionalized by it—or some (other) comfy hospital. My mind was filled with metaphors, all mixed. My life was a mixed metaphor. I was madly in love with business. Madly. I stepped back to contemplate its beauty and meaning. It was a big step. Then I took another. And another. With tears in my eyes I watched me leave business. . . .

The sounds are different now. The hum of air-conditioning no longer protects me. I hear what happens in the street: the rush of rubber on asphalt, horns, sirens, shouts, screams, laughter, brakes, car radios, crashes sometimes. . . . It's as though every day were Sunday—Sundays as they used to be when my wife took the children to the country and I worked alone among the impersonal sounds of the city, trying to disregard everything out there beyond the glass, and not answering the phone.

"Did anyone call?" she asked then—and asks now.

"I think so."

"What d'you mean? Who?"

"I don't know. I didn't answer."

"How can you do that, let the phone ring?"

"It's easy."

"Who d'you think it was?"

"I haven't any idea."

"Guess."

"If I cared I would have answered."

"It must've been——"

She gets busy calling friends. It's uncanny how she knows who would have called about what: this one to make a date, that one to break a date; one to complain, one to explain; one with gossip, one without. . . . When she spins the dial she can't lose. Either the other party did call, and she's right; or didn't, and she's not wrong, because this other party had something to say anyway, would have called if not so busy, meant to, was thinking of my wife—or me—or the children.

My wife, all by herself, is a potential research project in ESP. She receives messages before they are sent, picks up the phone before it rings. She is her own answering service. How redundant was that suggestion of mine to subscribe to such a service. How foolish. Now when I make a more radical suggestion—"Have the phone disconnected."—there's a look of terror in her eyes and nothing more for me to say. I wonder what frightens her, the calls she'd miss or the possibility no one would call. Anyway the phone is her pleasure. I use it only to save time. She uses the mail for that.

My secretary arrives at nine (theoretically nine—there's always that wait until the shoe drops with a foot inside it) and then (theoretically, again) there's silence. She has her instructions: to switch the phone extension from bell to light, to go through the mail, to disturb me only if there are important calls or letters, and otherwise to go ahead with what she can

do without me. That means mostly bills, bills of every variety,
ordinary bills, from bookstores and haberdashers; invoices
from suppliers and contractors (some subject to a 2% discount
if paid within ten days—she, too, my secretary works under
pressure); phone, gas, electric; insurance premiums; sub-
scription renewals; professional fees payable to the doctors,
dentists, lawyers, accountants, who keep me physically and
economically healthy; department store bills, complicated by
my wife's shopping habits ("Is it possible Mrs. —————
bought a dress, returned it, bought it again, and returned it
again—the same dress?" "Very possible." "You know, there's
a charge now for these pick-ups?" "There should be," I snap,
not really having hired her as an efficiency expert or comptrol-
ler. "All I wish," she snaps back, "is that Mrs.—————
would complete these transactions within one month, one bill-
ing period. It's difficult enough for me, I can imagine what it
is for the stores." "All part of the overhead," I reply with a
finality which gives the word a weight more like that of *over-
kill*.); monthly charge for burglar alarm maintenance; ditto
for real estate management; the children's schools, summer
camps. . . . All these and more have been flowing across her/
my/our desk along with bank statements, stockbrokers' state-
ments, withholding forms, tax forms, corporate reports, prox-
ies ("Just vote for Management, I don't want to see them."),
solicitations (a subject in itself) . . . . and more, again, more,
more, more . . . . a continuation of the flood that it was once
part of my job to deal with and divert to Corporate Giving (in
every sense) . . . .

The giving is personal now. The time is mine and not
the company's. And yet the world assumes I have more time,
am more available. Can one word like *solicitation*s even be-
gin to describe that mail, those calls? Their volume (in both

physical dimensions and decibels)? The variations in origin,
style, technique, motivation, etc., etc., etc.? Solicitations exist
in a context of etceteras, forgotten people, forgotten causes,
forgotten arts and sciences, all remembered by the remem-
bered rich, the people with names and spare etcetera time to
make the calls (or have them made), to stuff the envelopes (or
have them stuffed) . . . . I am overwhelmed by my popularity.
All this mail, all these calls, all, all are invitations, expres-
sions of love, from beginning to end. *We love you,* say the
stamps (rightside up or upside down). *We love you,* say the
signatures (slanting to left or right). *We love you,* say the
sound of the phone and then the voice at the other end of the
line. *How have you been? How are you? It's been a long
time. What I'm calling about is—*

They want me, or my wife, or both—and no doubt soon
our children will do—to serve on boards and committees and
councils; to sponsor and/or attend meetings, theatre benefits,
tours of homes and gardens; to join so-and-so and a few inter-
ested friends for lunch or cocktails or dinner in those same old
hotel ballrooms and suites (*no fund raising, just a few hours
of your time*); to help some young talent; to subscribe to such-
and-such new publication, dedicated to . . . . whatever. . . .

Spare me, I could scream, I don't want to go, I don't want
to see you, I don't want to see it, I don't want to hear it, I don't
want to read it. . . . But all I do is whisper that sometimes I
don't think they love me for myself.

I am on every list, the ones I was on in business and a
hundred more now where the compilers have been encouraged
by my new "spare time." Lists breed lists, and one yes pro-
vokes a dozen more requests. Once I received legitimate
alumni mail from the institutions (even businesses) which
educated me and gave me pleasure. Now I am an alumnus of

the lists themselves. . . . No catastrophe occurs locally, nation-
ally, or internationally of which I am not advised. Without
newspapers (or TV) I would still know all the bad things that
are happening. The world is delivered in the morning mail,
filled with wars, riots, earthquakes, droughts, floods (floods
within floods) . . . . My wife has her ESP; I have my CIA, out
there, with computers, gathering information and directing it
toward me.

For a while, as if I were still in business, as if I were
being paid to do it, I read all my mail. I was also interested
(as my wife is interested in the ringing of the phone). But
then, printed so expressively on glossy stock, that crippled
war orphan appeared just once too often, that little girl leaning
on her crutches and looking at me with dark hurt eyes staring
from a bruised face. Yes, I know that *I* had no right even to
think a complaint; I know what she would have given to be in
my place and receive my fat mail (perhaps containing a pic-
ture of me on my invisible crutches). I wanted to tell my sec-
retary to vote against Management, against God. Instead I
told her to screen my mail, sift it, strain it, filter it, and give
me only what's important, what comes from friends, the rarest
mail.

A simple directive. But there are other solicitations too,
the ones from book clubs, record clubs, travel clubs, political
clubs, sex clubs. . . . Yes, yes, yes again, I am on *every* list. I
always respond to the blanks on forms. I feel their emptiness,
their loneliness. I don't have the strength to say no. I need
the help of my secretary.

She helps, but is confused about what's important.
(Aren't we all? I ask compassionately.) Sometimes a personal
letter is buried under a pile of checks ready for signature
(with attached supporting invoices or solicitations) . . . .

Books and magazines come in faster than I can put them out
of the way (I no longer even try to read most of them), as
she keeps up with the two things: bills and charitable contribu-
tions. How I envy that British aristocracy which I'm told pays
its bills only once a year—and then a little late; and those
British banks which—as part of the service, a thank-you for
depositing funds—honor overdrafts. Yes, it must be a privi-
lege to receive mail (even bills), if you know you don't have
to reply, if no inner minority voice tells you you must. But
here there is that minority voice saying you are rich in an
alleged democracy, and "not working" in a land of work. Like
my wife, but perhaps on a grander scale, the only overdrafts
I'm permitted are those of guilt.

I would welcome a jury notice, a summons from some
state or county court, telling me that I'm wanted, needed (if
only for two weeks, every two years). In business such notices
went straight to the Legal Department, with a terse memo from
my desk, the desk of Mr. B., requesting postponement because
of pending negotiations, scheduled meetings, trips, any of a
dozen reasons important to me and therefore to the Legal De-
partment (though its bribes to the court were ultimately
treated by Accounting as unimportant—"petty cash," to be
exact). And now if I wanted it, which I don't, nothing I do
could justify a postponement. There would have to be some
external reason, perhaps a death in the family. . . No, I would
be there, in court, nine o'clock Monday morning, at the head
of the line with the other men who have retired (many of them
civil servants) and the women whose children have grown up
and left home (to fill better jobs than those their fathers
vacated). With them, this line of veterans, when challenged
by prosecution or defense to say what I do, I would tell them,
"Nothing." I would make them discover what once I did, what

once I had. . . But no notice comes. There's not even *that* acceptance. . . .

Before leaving—escaping—the subject of solicitations, I should whisper very very quietly that it's not all irritating, this pressure to give. There are pleasurable aspects: first, the recognition that one *can give* and, later, the recognition that one *has given.* That later recognition often takes the shape of—I whisper even more quietly now—privilege. Donations to hospitals are an investment in longevity; they are transformed into best rooms, the newest scarcest drugs and equipment, visits from chiefs of staff. Donations to schools become one's children's reservations. Donations to museums become invitations to gala opening parties. . . Everywhere one's name is on lists, in the very best, the very richest company: more gifts for the givers. . . . . Yes, as I once said, I would like to share the pride with which others receive fellowships, grants, etc. But, on second thought, there is pride, too, in giving. There are the joys, however subtle, of condescension. And, as we see, as we whisper, there are the rewards. . . .

Theoretically there's silence, but I do find myself around 9 A.M. listening for my secretary's footstep—just one, leading to the desk, but audible even on the carpet (in that little room adjoining mine, which once belonged to my wife). I hear purse, *Times* (a lump, intricately folded for subway travel), and bundle of mail drop, one by one, on the desk. I hear her settle into the swivel chair. I hear her letter opener cutting through paper, and sometimes the snip of scissors opening packages. She is really settled now, all set for work. . . . Her chair squeaks. She is up. The other shoe falls. She is on her way to the bathroom (my wife's, if it isn't occupied; down a flight to the one in the library, if it is). . . . . She is gone usually about ten minutes. Then again the step, the squeak. It is 9:30, and she is ready to begin, knowing she isn't to disturb me except for those important letters or calls (those dreams and fantasies!) . . . . First she types whatever manuscript I've left on her desk, perhaps five or six handwritten pages of what I choose to think of as economic whispers. This, my last day's work, will take her less than an hour—she is efficient, she gets my work out faster than I. During this period the steadiness of her typing is soothing, protective as once was central air-conditioning. I work best now, while her rhythm is regular, before the stops and starts of paying bills, dues, tuitions. . . the silences between checks . . . silences the opposite of "pregnant" . . . empty silences, waiting for a word or words from me. Yes, she waits for my work, even if now the world doesn't. I feel her in the next room, waiting.

What do I write? It *is* difficult to explain—I am not being coy with my wife—I am not sure it can be explained except by examples. I write what one would expect from a man without a memory, a man whose preference is the present tense. For history to exist it must be recorded. Bibliographies, anthologies, catalogues, journals exist for me only if I hold them in my hand—or eye—or ear. Ink on paper, needle in groove, impression on tape, oil on canvas . . . without these I cannot remember what I've read, seen, heard, felt, touched . . . the day's, today's, my day's fluctuations, measured within an eighth of a point, a tenth of a degree . .

I collect the words of Gresham, Smith, Malthus, Ricardo, Saint-Simon, Proudhon, Fourier, Marx, Engels, George, Veblen, Keynes . . . measuring the molten mass of their precious shimmering words against those of other poets. Shakespeare, for example: *There's no true drop of blood in him, to be truly touched with love. If he be sad, he wants money.* And: *There is money; spend it, spend it; spend more; spend all I have;*

only give me so much of your time in exchange of it . . . And:
One business does command us all; for mine / is money. And,
and, and,—The Plays are a torrent of gold, silver, copper.
How many times does Iago say *Put money in thy purse?* I
marvel at the clarity of that command. In all economic/poetic
literature I know of nothing to compare, except perhaps Jon-
son's *I will pronounce the happy word, Be rich.*

William Shakespeare, Ben Jonson—yes, yes, I raise my
voice, but no more than for Sir Thomas Gresham, Adam
Smith, Thomas Robert Malthus, David Ricardo, and the rest:
my classics, my pantheon, the poets' corner of my bookshelf.

And that other William, just as sweet, Blake, blessed
Blake: *The Female searches land and sea for gratifications to
the / Male genius, who in return clothes her in gems and gold /
And feeds her with the food of Eden; hence all her beauty
beams.* Ha, when they say Blake was a visionary, a visionary
realist is what they mean (or should) a visionary realist/econ-
omist.

The Bible, too, I love (no more or less). Gold flows there
also, and I write about it. I have tortured these words of
Isaiah:

> *Wherefore do ye spend money for that which is not
> bread? And your labor for that which satisfieth not?
> Hearken diligently unto me, and eat ye that which is
> good and let your soul delight in fatness.*

and they have tortured me. I have written an essay, one that
will perhaps make me famous, about Isaiah, man of extremes,
cranky and lovable, harsh and sentimental, torn between Old
Testament realism and New Testament idealism, prophet of
economic ambivalence, my spiritual father on the edge of an
abyss filled with money, another visionary who, like me, saw
things just a little out of focus. How could he have envisaged

a world so technologically advanced, so rich that bread would be taken for granted and choices made, not between necessities, but luxuries: a world in which bread itself became the hip word for money and *that* tasteless bread, not the labor for it, the only satisfaction? How? How could he have known the world I left? I think of my former colleagues at their jobs, increasingly more monotonous, more specialized, more distant from end products—and from pleasure too (or satisfaction, as Isaiah called it)—all for the compensation of longer nights and weekends and vacations in which to spend the money accumulated during working hours, to let it, this economic surplus, sift through the economy, as tips mostly, crumbs from the bread, little tastes sometimes of icing from the cake. . .

Bread should be *fat*—that would be a better, hipper word. "Hey, Man, lay some fat on me." Money is an abstraction (see my whisper #7), a metaphor for what people want and what they have to give. Money has nothing to do with money.

Our children, in their pre-inflationary innocence, sing:
A penny for a spool of thread,
A penny for a needle—
That's where the money goes,
Pop goes the weasel!

I compose this reply:

Ninety thou for a country house,
Two hundred for one in the city—
That's where the money goes,
Down to the nitty-gritty.

Yes, nursery rhymes, popular songs (*Pennies from Heaven, Jimmy Had a Nickel, Ten Cents a Dance, Brother,*

Can you Spare a Dime, I've Got Five Dollars, We're in the Money, Million Dollar Baby: another essay, a history of the Depression), phrases from advertising copy and legal documents—all these are grist for my economic mill. In leases, too, I find poetry, particularly in that clause called "Quiet Enjoyment." And in dictionary definitions. Just a few hours ago I was wondering about those decibels I hear ringing all the time and discovered they are *units for measuring the volume of a sound, equal to the logarithm of the ratio of the intensity of an arbitrarily chosen standard sound.* Arbitrarily I have chosen my standard sound, given it a name, called it a whisper for lack of a more technical term, and wonder now if, beyond this, silence exists.

Does absolute silence exist the way justice is supposed to, beyond the apparent random phenomena, beyond the noisy bumping of particles? When my bibliographical/anthological method fails, I turn to my own words, write my own laws:

A man's unhappiness is the measure of his worth and rights.

A man's pay shall be directly proportionate to his dislike for his work.

The most unhappy shall lead.

Shit is an acquired taste.

These, the product of my business years, my years of primary research, I call General Laws of Compensation. My secretary types them in a few seconds, files them under C, where they will wait until, by some accretive process, they join enough other words to become that tome I envisage, now tentatively titled *Fat*, my counter-revolutionary *Das Kapital.* (I note *Kapital* with a *K* looks steadier than with a *C*. Like *Kultur* with a *K*. . . . Both feet on the ground. . . Those Germans!)

Their books, my book!—and I have not yet mentioned

the book I love maybe most of all, one that comes from thous-
ands of different publishers in thousands of different editions,
bound or unbound, hard- or soft-cover, the greatest collabora-
tive book of all time, truly a work of participatory literature,
a do-it (or undo-it)-yourself, infinitely expandable (or con-
tractable), horizontal (or vertical), multi-media, multi-track
masterpiece in which energy assumes a million disguises and
time, place, size, even authorship are all subject to change.
    Here is a typical page:

	No.	
	.... 19	$\frac{1\text{-}67}{210}$
Pay to the order of .... $...............................		
.... Dollars		
TRUST COMPANY		
....		

By itself, this may look like nothing; but repeated again
and again, the pages have a cumulative impact; a rhythm
builds, not unlike that of life. . . O, check book, darling of my
library, I drool and dribble at the thought of spreading your
pages . . . making deposits and withdrawals . . . balancing you
on the tip of my ball-point pen. . .
    Even if I don't know precisely what I'm doing, doing it
makes time pass. How can I answer my wife's questions now
any more than when I was in business? Then I might have said
I was changing energy into money. Now I suppose I'm chang-
ing it back again. Writing, without a deadline, without a defi-

nite purpose, is a luxury. I don't even want to reform any-
thing—except my own thoughts.

I change along with the style of my life. Different work-
ing clothes indicate a different man. Anonymity cannot, as
once I thought, be bought. In theory what one buys is privacy.
In practice that privacy attracts attention. Not only those best
tables and best seats, which once I whispered of, but best beds,
best rooms, best parties, best collections . . . What can be
bought, it turns out, is a sort of *identity in things*, and then
only death can restore one's anonymity. True, the rich defy
it more comfortably in their so-called "private rooms" (at-
tended by specialists and nurses 'round the clock), have these
rooms named for them—or that wing, or the hospital itself—
in gestures of familial gratitude for extra days on earth,
where they were known and their reservations honored. It's
difficult to accept one grave being no better than the next. No
grave is best. . . Even pyramids get robbed or disappear.

I don't condescend to my fellow rich, pharaonic friends.
My therapy—death therapy, I suppose—is economic too. As
my wife said, I shop. She's wrong, though about this not
being research. I search, research, and search again for my-
self in clothes; for the fabric, the cut, the accessory that's me.
Me, visible in my invisibility. Me, visible only to myself. . .
The search is endless—hopeless, in that sense—but fun. Like
writing and business, shopping passes time. Decisions must
be made: this phrase or that, this contract or that, this material
or that. . . I can spend hours, do spend them, deciding upon
width of lapel, flare of pants cuffs, treatment of darting in bold
plaid sport jacket (losing pattern vs. losing fit: a crisis!) . . .
and yet, even while making these subtle decisions, I know that
all fashionability leads to invisibility, that only I will see the
nakedness of each stitch. I go to tailors, bootmakers, haber-

dashers as once I might have gone to buy armor.

In business I wore suits and relaxed after hours in sports clothes appropriate to my craft: the blazer with gold buttons, the straight gray flannels, the dazzling tie or scarf. Now, working by day in sweater and slacks, at night I like to dress up, not down. I am in the midst of fittings for a third tuxedo, a simple suit, a 15-ounce black cavalry twill detailed so quietly its wide belt loops and Western pockets will barely whisper—unless I should have reach to reach for money. No busy snappy thumbs under suspenders, no bright braces (to use my pseudo-British tailor's word)—no, not for me. Once again I move toward invisibility, that world of dark suits toward which I've always moved. I was doing it in business, I do it now—but at a different time of day. Now I shop *in* sports clothes, not only *for* them. Always I've worn secrets. Clothes are secrets that can be kept for at least a season.

In business I wore my "tuxedo" to the office, just as I shaved *in the morning*. My wife must have loved me then, when she didn't see me at work but knew I was clean, fresh, well turned out. Now mornings I'm a dirty useless thing. Well, that too is why I go to tailors and the rest, to make myself beautiful, if not useful. . . Sometimes to be beautiful means to be useless. I'm not thinking only of the fashion world, but of "wasted" space in art and architecture, "wasted" words in books, "wasted" sounds and silences in music, "wasted" movement in dance . . . all aspects of "wasted" energy, translated into space and time. . . Waste turns out to be as basic to definitions of art as to those of business.

My wife says, "I know we're not poor, I know we don't really *miss* your salary, it's just that we *saved* money when you didn't have time to shop."

The words sound sharply familiar, an echo of her friends

telling her to get a job or take up a serious hobby or worthy cause. I re-echo, "Why don't *you* get a job?"

She has her reasons, a whole catalogue of them, beginning with the children, moving through this house in the city and the summer place we finally stopped dreaming about and bought ("jointly and severally"), and Ruby . . . moving, moving to me. Yes, my wife throws me at me.

"Who would fix your lunch?"

"Ruby."

"Who would you complain to, if I weren't around?"

"No one."

"Who would answer the doorbell on Ruby's day off?"

"Beryl."

My secretary's name—I knew it would come out—I'm surrounded by jewels. I was hoping Beryl would accept economics as a form of fiction, but I lost control, and now she should know it's real; it, including all the laws, theories, abstractions, formulae, symbols on ticker tape . . . all real . . .

What's not real—I might as well tell her, since she's the first to read my thoughts—is these conversations with my wife (her identity will not be divulged, must remain a mystery as it is to me). No, we're not really talking about her getting a job or my returning to business. No, what we're talking about is the *function* of money, money as energy, once again—we're mining at a level close to that of sex. What I want Beryl to understand is that men and women represent two different economic theories. (And I remind her, these theories are *real*.) Even now, this late in the game, the woman watches the cave, saves, sews, cooks, makes things nice, while the man goes out and hunts. Maybe that's what my wife's bitching is about, that I'm not out hunting—anyway, not early enough in the day. She knows that for women, money's a noun; for men, a verb.

Women have not got past shopping and hoarding. Men under-
stand capitalized values; pyramiding, not just pyramids; bal-
looning, not just balloons. The sexuality of capital!— there's
a theme, another truffle in the paté to be packed in *Fat!* When
I'm out shopping, feminine as that may seem (even in a coun-
try of men pushing carts around supermarts), I am out, I am
useful. I help render the fat. I watch it drip into a bigger
gravy bowl than mine. I see the speed with which it falls
through strata of the economy. I like fast money better than
slow institutional trickles. Buy six suits in an hour and you've
done something. If, in the afternoon, the money isn't moving
fast enough, one must prod it like an afternoon date (with sec-
retary or anyone) . . . The idea is to be useful, to waste aggres-
sively.

In business the sense of waste was exhilarating. Then I
devoured the space my office occupied and my secretary's
portion of the executive corridor, all those cubic feet of condi-
tioned air we were fed, all those foot-candles of illumination
at desk level, all those muted decibels, quires of stationery . . .
duplicates, triplicates, quadruplicates, polyplicates . . . stapled
. . . enveloped . . . addressed . . . sent by messengers, postmen,
pilots . . . to those who glanced and crushed my words into a
ball.

Now what sense of productive waste do I have? A pack
or two of cigarettes in the morning. A few sheets of a yellow
pad. The revolutions of a ball point pen. Some paper clips.
One carbon copy (in case *the editor*, an abstraction out there,
should lose the original). After four or five hours: a sandwich,
a beer, a paper napkin—two, if there's a lot of mayonnaise in
the tunafish.

Compare this piddling waste with the steam turbines
once spinning to feed air and light to me and my secretary,

chain saws cutting down whole forests to furnish some waiting
world with copies of my words, men racing 'round the globe
to deliver those words to the folks in the International Division
(even if they did crush them into balls) . . . Only shaving is
still satisfyingly wasteful: the water, the soap, the cream, the
blade, the lotion, the Q-tip for lather that lingers in the ears. . .

I'm not really sure if I hunt in the morning or the after-
noon, but I do know that the afternoon's catch is noticed more.
After all, the morning's is private, something between me and
my (private) secretary. But in the afternoon. . . Say, someone
admires my tie—perhaps that bold one with green and blue
stripes, which I still cherish. . .

"Where'd you get it?" he/she asks.

Would it make any sense to say I don't know, to lift it
from that 36+ paunch, look at it incredulously, and read the
name on the label (the way in boyhood, and again in business,
I was taught to)? No, the unconscious male is a myth encom-
passing the absent-minded professor, the artist too preoccu-
pied to think about those things, the busy businessman. . . No,
every man, if he is wearing a tie, knows which, where he
bought it or who gave it to him.

I return from shopping (my therapeutic walk). I am tired
now. I have worked since early morning. I prepare for a nap:
pile books and magazines on the night table, turn on the
bedlamp, turn off the phone, open the window, pull down the
blinds, close the bedroom door.

"When you take a nap, I can't even get into my own bed-
room."

"Why would you want to?"

"I might need something. I might want to change. I might
want to do my hair."

"I told you we should add to the house—or move."

"I like this house. I like it the way it is—"

This conversation has been going for several years. Recently my wife was inspired to add: "Isn't it wrong to save office rental? Think what you could spend, not only on rent, but fixing up an office, the way you want, corklined and all." She smiled, telling me with her moist lips and gleaming caps that she understood my economic theories, was willing to let me express them—outside the house.

Now, in bed between cool sheets, as I read this financial review, that newsletter; study their pictures of the economy; climb heroic peaks, descend to gloomy troughs, begin the climb again; expand and contract with the bars on graphs; cut pies into unequal slices... the images blur, my mind blurs. I am thinking about the apartment house being completed just down the block. I am furnishing a three-room unit. I am re-creating an environment I once knew. There's no cork, but there's acoustic tile on the ceiling and heavy carpet on the floor. And there's built-in air-conditioning, shiny desks and files, walls painted an institutional menthol . . . My mind is tired. My eyes are tired. I turn off the light and drift into that cool green womb.

The nap is brief but refreshing, full of air-conditioned dreams. Downstairs I hear my wife and daughter (my son has not yet returned from school). I buzz them on intercom to say that I'm up, that the bedroom is available. I hear my daughter already racing up the stairs. I tell my wife, "I accept your eviction notice."

"What does that mean?"

"I'll get an apartment down the street."

"You don't have to," she replies, "I don't really mind not being able to get into the bedroom, or Beryl being in my dressing room, or having to fix lunch—"

Thus she begins to list the things she doesn't mind, but I have to cut her off—my daughter has arrived with a kiss. She tells me about that day's visit to a computer center as once I told my parents about a school trip to the planetarium. Then, like most days, she sits on my bed with my pillow propped behind her and watches me do my exercises, a ten-minute routine (mostly jogging in place) intended to make up for the lost movement and action of business.

As I'm finishing, she says, "You do the same thing every day, don't you?"

"Not exactly," I mutter between push-ups.

"Oh yes. You get up. You have breakfast. You read the paper. You work. You have lunch. You shop. You take a nap. You do your exercise. You read. You have dinner. You go to bed."

"Some afternoons I have appointments. Some nights Mommy and I go out."

"But *usually* you do the same thing."

"Yes."

She is hardly old enough to remember when each day I went romantically off to business. My son remembers. He still says sometimes that he wants to be a businessman. He used to like coming to the office, where my secretary and others along the corridor made a fuss over him, gave him office supplies. But now, sometimes, too, he says he wants to be an economist. I don't encourage him in this identification with my present life—I'm not sure he would like it.

I quote something to him, which I heard on the radio: "Thin may be in, but fat's where it's at."

"What program was that?" my son asks skeptically.

"I don't know. Probably something I heard in a cab or on the way to the country."

He studies me.

I smile.

"*You* wrote it," he says triumphantly.

"I wish I had," I reply, knowing even then that I would eventually (now!) and knowing that historical priority is meaningless to a child.

Just as it is to me. If originality is being oneself, that must include quoting what one wants: a form of banking, a way of withdrawing deposits.

The thought that I can pass such wisdom on to my son is cheering. It makes me feel like Lord Chesterfield.

In my journal I make two entries:

Was it Cocteau (again!) who said the drama of opium is simply that of comfort and discomfort? The drama of money is the same. Money, the opium of people.

I fear a time will come when I have enough clothes, enough books, enough everything, a time when my days (my afternoons, in particular) will be empty in their fulness.

The phone rings. It is one of those calls that still come from former business associates, including the man I broke in (as they say) to replace myself. These calls I take, in order to explain agreements, written or unwritten, made years ago by me on behalf of the company.

"The intent was—" I begin, trying to remember words spoken, with mouths full, so long ago at some elite luncheon club.

At the other end of the line, my replacement probes, asks questions, trying to pin down the understanding. He is well-trained, quick with numbers, precision-tooled. I have the feeling that I am speaking to some lost part of myself.

hers: #10

Wow! Sometimes you get more than you ask for. Words anyway, if not direct answers. He has more time than I do—I always knew that.

I asked bluntly if he really thinks these whispers, or drippings of fat, or whatever he's calling them have anything to do with economics.

"Can't you accept the family as the basic economic unit?" he replied, once again answering a question with a question.

Then he handed me this (neatly typed, as always, by Beryl):

Fable

Two artists (close friends, who early in their careers shared a studio) dreamt and talked of immortality, almost letting this dream distract them from their work, and indeed permitting much of their energy to be dissipated in visions of their future, even posthumous, reputations. But somehow between discussions and arguments about the different routes to fame, the work was done.

One believed that by putting all of himself into his work he could never die; and now, years since his death, he has his immortality. His joy, his intelligence, his strength, his calm are all there in his work—along with his pain, his stupidity, his weakness, his rage.

And he wonders sometimes if a different dream might not have been better. The pain, lingering and endless, particularly bothers him.

The other kept himself out of his work, thinking he could only confine it. He wanted to create something far grander and better organized than himself, a world like that of Oriental gardens, a susurrant world of pine needles and rocks and water.

His work, too, has lasted and become institutionalized. Scholars study it, lifting rocks, uprooting plants, filtering water in their search for him.

And they are successful. They find not only him, but his close friend, and even friends of friends. The garden is crowded now with everything he excluded—ruthlessly, they say. He is bothered most by the lost calm, the intrusion of rage.

The two old friends, having completed their work, only talk now. They talk mostly about new dreams of anonymity. And sometimes, because they are such old friends, they admit that they see themselves in each other's work.

What am I supposed to make of this? Those two "artists," are they artists, or partners in business, or partners in life, or what? Am I wrong, or is my husband once again writing about us? Surely, if life is an art, marriage is one of its most complex forms. . .

I re-read the fable, assuming this time that he is one artist and I am the other. Now things begin to fall in place. That shared studio: the small apartment in which we lived before we were married. Those dreams and talks of immortality: his determination to be a success in business, mine to raise a family. . . We did talk then, in the early years just before and after marriage. But it was he who decided to put everything into his work, to invest there so completely that nothing was left for himself—or me. Originally, in my work, I held back. I thought of that first apartment as a place to talk and sleep—a place to fuck. Only when we moved (to a second, larger apartment) did I begin to buy cookbooks, good-design award-winning appliances, antiques . . . all arranged with some care . . . Only then did I begin to cultivate my Oriental garden (as he calls it). And not until our son was born and we moved to the brownstone did the exact placement of things, the timing of meals, the metronomic rhythm of life become a reality, my reality, our reality.

He taught me about systems, and I taught him about life—with the help of our children. A world of whispers is a fantasy. Screams and howls are part of life—children teach us that.

He wouldn't have given me this so-called fable if he didn't want my comments. All right: I'm not sure I like his voice when it's given this much shape, as though he was speaking through some timeless telephone. I like a harsher, more immediate ring. . . . And since, so obviously, he's asking for criticism: I do prefer the real world of things—words actually spoken, photographs, documents. . . Abstractions are part of a male world I've never understood; they come from Seats on the New York Stock Exchange and Seats of Higher Learning. . . . He may think they're real, but he can't tell me that we see ourselves in each other's work. I wish he'd tell me instead that, after twenty years, we fit better than ever. The cock may be systematic, the pussy lives

I got this far, sitting at the library desk, sipping dry vermouth (no gin, I swear) as I caress my rickety imported portable, with its squared-off telegraphic typeface and pigskin carrying case: a gift, once long ago, from him: a toy compared with that heavy steady efficient electric machine of Beryl's, and yet of course a thing of love.

The last sentence before the break must have been inspired—or provoked—by his footsteps on the stair. (The children are in bed—it's not often I have the library to myself.) My pinky was poised kittenishly above the period I didn't touch, when he entered the room, leaned over my shoulder, and began to read. (This is a right he expects, while I wait until he *gives* me *his* words.) He was silent for some time. Then, in a razor-sharp chrome-edged whisper, he began:

"Do you really think what I wanted was criticism?"

"Yes. A reaction. A response. *Something.*"

"A judgment?"

"Maybe."

"You're wrong. At the most, a discernment. *Positive* criticism, *if that exists.*"

"My comments *are* positive."

"About my voice being too shapely, too abstract? What I want is for you to love what I do, to accept it, *everything.*"

"I do, I do, but—"

"Without buts. Without analysis. . . . Neither of those 'artists' have anything to do with you. They're both me."

"But you have something to do with me. You're part of me, and I'm part of you."

He smiled, turned my words into song, frugged around the library, chanting "You're part of me. / I'm part of you. / Come on, baby, / Why don't we screw."

"Not funny!" I said emphatically, and turned back to my typewriter.

He kissed me on the neck. I pretended not to notice. I got

as far as *I got this far, sitting at the library desk, sipping dry vermouth (no gin, I swear) as I caress*. . . His tongue was in my ear, *my rickety* was in my head. . .

". . . Why don't we. . ."

The fact is I preferred to, rather than listen to him sing.

It's the next morning. The children have gone to school. He's gone to his office. Beryl's gone to hers (*mine*, but all that's about to end soon—a lease is being drawn on the apartment down the block). I'm in the library again. (By now Beryl may be in my bathroom, doing whatever she does there, with my perfume—but that, too, is about to end.) I hate this room, find it the strangest, most hostile environment in the house. You understand, this is not his working library, nor mine. The books on economics, the poetry, the reference volumes are upstairs in his office and in a bookshelf by his side of the bed; the cookbooks are in the kitchen. This room, this library, is only a storage bin for things he has already read or may someday want to read. Except for the door entering the room and the wall of windows on the street, every inch is books, like so many scalps or trophies hung on the walls, three of which would be back another foot if it weren't for this bulk of words.

This room is a found environment. No doubt, previous owners of the house had different books, but the shelves were here. I can see them as they must have looked in Teddy Roosevelt's time: more sets, darker bindings, but still a load of words, read and unread. This room could be bright, cheerful, easy to clean. Instead, Ruby climbs the ladder, holding that long vacuum-cleaner extension, and sucks dust from the spines of these enemies of mine, these motley ranks which have taken him from me, claimed his time, and will again. . . . And my time. And Ruby's. All he notices is a book out of place or dustjacket torn.

Besides storage, the only use this room has is for coffee after dinner (or in the morning, like now). But after dinner the room really works. It's a three-dimensional Rorschach. There are always those cultured ladies who must study each title, craning their necks to find some they recognize and can comment on. And there are the sharp-eyed athletic males who scurry up the ladder to grab something they've heard about but haven't read. Odd, how willingly my husband lends his books or gives them away—sometimes in a spirt of sharing what he likes; sometimes, I suppose, just to make more space. But whether lent or given, the books seldom return; they are replaced by others. The flow, as he says, is endless. The flow of words, silent, whispered, bound. . . There are some who don't read the titles at all. For them, the neat narrow vertical rectangles of color become an overall textured pattern, a sort of deep-carved wallpaper which "reads" *cozy library* or something of the sort. They tell me it's a charming room, that the Tiffany lamp picks up the colors of the books—or vice versa. I'd like to show them what this room could really be. I'd like to replace this wallpaper with something practical and pretty. I'd like to wash all the words off the walls.

hers: #11

That was some weeks ago. I was in the library then. I am
now. While I typed I was drinking vermouth and, later, coffee.
As I type now, I am drinking coffee, my third cup. Perhaps I
shouldn't have so much: it seems to agitate me; it is my liquid
Rorschach, my Rorschach now within a Rorschach. Coffee
even looks like ink, the way I take it, strong and black.

Black. What a color to start the day with. But not inap-
propriate. Here I am on the dark side of the house, banished
from my sunny dressing room, while my husband and his sec-
retary work—or play—upstairs. Well, they move to that new
apartment in about a month. I can't wait.

After today's newspapers, I re-read what I wrote that
night and morning, seemingly long ago. I can hardly believe
the strident sound of my voice. It's as if the recording equip-
ment—this beloved old typewriter of mine—was defective.
This isn't such a terrible room, but I must have thought so then.
If I didn't recognize the typeface, I'd think my husband had
edited what I wrote, organized and systematized it into some
weird delusion. But of course that's unlikely: he loves this
room, thinks only that it's in the wrong place, that it should be
next to his office. Perhaps, when he moves, these books will go
with him.

I wonder if maybe the quiet rage I was in had anything
to do with this room. . . . I cannot recapture my mood. That's
why I've started a new whisper. Maybe the other would have

gone on to what I'll write now; I don't know.

Once my husband made what he called a "rather unseemly confession." He spoke of his piles: "There, at the very core of what's left of my body, I am most vulnerable, most tender, most pained." And he continued: "Perhaps piles acquire a disproportionate significance when they belong to you—everything does. Especially pain."

That's enough of an introduction. I have my piles, too: the children. And it's no comfort whatsoever to know that other mothers have theirs. If anything, communal agony is just a bigger pain in the ass. Yes, I see these other mothers at the children's school, and at cocktail parties and dinners. I listen to their woeful tales of insecurity, sibling rivalry, underachievement, identity crises. . . the whole tired jargon-ridden vocabulary. . . I listen, but I rarely speak. I am ashamed. Even now, after going for more than a year to that doctor to whom we were referred by the school ("Your children are bright enough, but they seem disturbed, unable to concentrate, unable to keep up with their work and organize it. . ."), I blame myself, consider the children *my* job.

We go as a family, twice a week, Wednesdays at four and Saturdays at nine. I don't know why I mention the times. They no longer seem the most inconvenient hours. The doctor has pointed out that one hour later on Wednesdays would really have cut into cocktails and that on Saturday he has a session at eight. True, true, we are neither the first nor the last, I see the other families waiting in the reception room or leaving as we enter. I try not to look at them. I try not to let them look at me.

Session! Wednesday session! Saturday session! sometimes additional sessions!—the word hisses in my mind, another part of that special vocabulary in which hours don't exist. Not even fifty-minute hours. No, if the doctor is on time—running on schedule, he calls it—there's still a little game to be played. The waiting game. A children's game, the object of which is to see (hear) who'll speak first. The doctor never does. That seems to be against the rules. He smokes his pipe. He coughs. He scratches the hairy parts of his body. He makes notes on a pad. (About us? I wonder. Or the previous patients? Or is he simply catching up on correspondence?) He makes my husband seem positively loquacious.

Our daughter breaks the silence: "Why don't we talk about what he did last night?" She points at her brother.

"What'd I do?" he replies.

And we're off on a dialogue that can last the next forty-five minutes, forty-five sessions, or forty-five years. . .

"You farted in my face—that's what you did."

"And what had you done?" The doctor finally speaks.

"I didn't do anything."

"Oh, no. She just bit me, that's all. Right on the ass. I can show you the teethmarks—" He starts to open his belt.

The doctor indicates that won't be necessary. "And then?" he asks.

"And then, of course, *she* begins screaming at me."

"*She* screamed at me too."

"*She* screamed louder at me."

"*She* gets madder at me."

She is me. I've had enough cues. I'm on stage: "What am I *supposed* to do? I can't even make myself be heard without screaming."

"It's *the way* she screams," our son—*his* son—says. "She's always swearing at us. She called us a pair of fucking brats."

It's true, I did. I look at the doctor for disapproval. No

reaction. Approval maybe? I did *express* myself. Still no re-
action. His face is blank. I turn to my husband, sitting on the
couch beside me (that's the way we're divided today; some
days our daughter is next to me; and he and our son sit in the
chairs across the room). I detect disapproval in my husband's
expression, rigidity in the set of his mouth, a lack of respons-
iveness as his eyes meet mine. He has told me that I mustn't
swear at the children; that if I do, I can't expect them to speak
nicely to me.

"I don't remember Mommy saying that," our daughter
comes to my rescue.

Now the doctor's mouth opens. "Are you sure?" he asks,
staring hard at our little girl until quite feebly she shakes her
head from side to side.

Just as I'm drowning in guilt, certain that once again the
doctor has sided with my husband and son against me and my
daughter, the doctor comes to my rescue.

"Where were *you* during all of this?" he asks my hus-
band.

"I was in my study, working."

"And you heard nothing?"

"It's an old house, post-and-beam construction, open
stairwell—I hear eveything."

"But you prefer not to get involved?"

"With the screaming?"

"With the children."

"After dinner they have their work, and I have mine."

"That's a very neat arrangement: you take care of your
work, your wife takes care of the discipline. She screams to
avoid giving them the love they're asking for, and you seclude
yourself, you're never quite there." The doctor looks at his
watch. Our time is up. As he stands to usher us out, he

says, "I think we've made real progress today. Don't stop now. Continue this at home. *Ventilation* is important. I'd like to see the two of you alone before our next regular session."

We arrange an appointment, an *irregular* session. I know what that'll be like—more of the same. He'll probe, trying once again to discover the lack of *structure* in our lives. He wonders if my husband really works; if dropping out, being "retired" at such an early age isn't a bad example for the children. And he wonders if I cook, as I say I do; if that, and the house, and the children, and my husband, and I myself, can really keep me busy all day long. He'll paint some gloomy statistical picture of some gloomy statistical American family in which the husband is weak and the wife is strong. And he'll try to get my husband to scream. And once again he won't succeed.

At our last private irregular session, my husband told him in a whisper, "D'you know why I'm strong? Because I lean on my wife." He laughed as though the laugh too was whispered, but the doctor didn't get the joke. "She's strong enough to defend me against the phone, the children, invitations. . . And my secretary takes care of the mail. . . Maybe she should come to one of these sessions."

"And Ruby," I added.

"You've told me Ruby sides with your daughter when the children fight. What about the secretary?"

"Beryl sides with my husband."

Again he whispered a laugh, and I responded, though more raucously. We moved closer together on the couch, so close our bodies were kissing. The doctor's pipe dropped from his mouth. Whether from surprise or fatigue is impossible to say.

The phone's been ringing constantly. Nice calls, but—
my husband's right—distracting to someone attempting to
write. One friend wants the recipe for my caviar ring. I'd bet-
ter do that now. (I insert carbon paper and extra sheet of sta-
tionary.)

Caviar en Gelée (for 12)

2½ tablespoons gelatine
4 cups chicken broth
8 ounces caviar
6 hard-boiled eggs
1 bunch watercress
1 pint sour cream

*Dissolve gelatine in chicken broth over low flame. Spread
caviar evenly into oiled 6-cup ring mold. Pour ½ cup broth
over caviar. Refrigerate.*

*Separately mince whites and yolks of eggs. When gela-
tine has set on caviar, spread egg whites evenly, add another
½ cup broth, and refrigerate again. When egg-white layer has
set, repeat process with egg yolks. When egg-yolk layer has
set, fill mold with remaining aspic broth. Refrigerate 1 hour.
Unmold carefully. Garnish center of ring with tops of water-
cress. Serve with toast; sour cream on the side.*

Tablespoons, cups, ounces . . . small easy numbers . . .
here's a vocabulary I understand, a finite vocabulary . . . like
that of my husband's *$18,000,000 @ 7½%* . . . even like
that of the doctor's bills, if not his working lingo. . .

(Oops! I forgot to remove the carbon copy. I'll cut off
everything that follows "sour cream on the side." *La crême
aigre à coté,* in French cookbooks, written by White Russians

in that vocabulary I understand in every language. . . . My Chinese fortune cookie contains a French recipe. My Japanese fortune cookie contains a photograph of a couple making love. My Italian fortune cookie contains a Chinese fortune cookie. Boxes within boxes within boxes. . . Rorschachs within Rorschachs. . . I'm on my fifth cup of coffee. . .

"Allo!" The phone again. A market research firm wanting to know what I'm watching on television. "Vous croyez que je n'ai rien de mieux à faire de mon temps?" I hang up on the startled static at the other end of the line. Ha! my husband laughs in whispers, I laugh in French. If it had been one o'clock, I might have been watching *The Galloping Gourmet*, the one lively program on day-time TV. I like him, that Australian Mr. Kerr, *Le Gourmet Galopante, Le Galo Gourmetante*. . . I like his having a sense of humor about food. It's *not* all that serious. Onions will do when leeks are not available, and almost any wild mushroom will replace cèpes (*Boletus edulis*) . . . I like his drinking while he cooks. A bit of the highball he holds in his hand, when what's called for is sherry. Yes! Did I mention that since the fourth cup of coffee I've been adding brandy? Well, I have. And I understand—*like*—that too: drinking while writing.

Once Ruby was emptying my husband's waste basket into the garbage can outside our house, and there were two empty whiskey bottles in it among the hundreds of cigarette butts and crushed balls of paper. She said, "God bless him!"

At that time I wasn't sure what she meant: God protect him? Or God praise him? I asked her.

"Oh, Ah don' know," she said, fidgeting, "Ah jus' mean he work so hard.")

What an extravagant pair of parentheses, containing so much. I feel them surrounding me like my husband's arms.

Despite the phone, despite the wobbling wheels in my mind (turning now in this stream of coffee and brandy), I have a destination, questions to ask toward which I've been moving:

1. Why hasn't my husband considered psychiatry as an economic phenomenon?

2. Doesn't he recognize it as a magnificent example of his favorite theme, money trickling through the economy?

3. (a) Hasn't he noticed how much better the doctor is dressing? (b) Is it possible he is going to my husband's tailor?

Other questions occur to me. My mind is filled with questions. This writing game is not easy. It is tiring. I, too, will have a light lunch and take a nap—if I can get in the bedroom.

When my husband was speaking of his piles, he also said, "It's nothing really, just part of life." He's always doing that, wearing that casual detached mask. I can't. *It's something really*, the children—the largest part of my life, divided as it is in thirds.

his: #11

Bowwow! I respond, salivating like one of Pavlov's dogs, as I answer her questions:

1. Because psychiatry is peripheral, not a basic industry.

2. Yes, it is an example of money trickling through the economy. Deductible money. But hardly a "magnificent" example. Even medical doctors have elastic sessions—and elastic fees. So do all technicians. But I still maintain that *the* magnificent example is lawyers. They stretch words further than psychiatrists. And they spend money, like words, more quickly, more generously.

3. (a) He isn't dressing better. He doesn't dress. He wears costumes. Off the peg, like his ideas. Unrelated to anything else. Without a context. Have you ever noticed his shirt, tie, belt, socks, shoes? What happens to your critical intelligence at these sessions? If a woman failed this way, you'd know. Treat your doctor as an equal.

(b) There's no possibility. Try to follow one of those fashionably bold patterns he now wears—down from the collar to the jacket skirt or pants cuff. Nothing follows, which is to say everything does, like the points in an argument against ready-made clothes. I wish he'd charge more, if only to dress better, this Freudian fee-losopher of ours.

Our life at the doctor's is about the same as at any other time—the usual mixture of silence and sound. It isn't even

more expensive. It costs us, the family, the same $40 per hour
at a good restaurant or a sporting event. But perhaps again my
wife will say I'm wearing that casual cool detached mask. Do
you know what's behind that mask? A face, casual, cool, and
detached.

his: #12

Does that count, my #11? It was really a hurried note, written to my wife the first day Beryl and I occupied this new apartment. I thought she'd be amused by it and by my *mailing* it. She wasn't. Not by either. . . . Or perhaps my mistake was enclosing a change-of-address card. . . Anyway, #11 was, until now, the last thing I wrote. Since then, for more than a week, I've been unpacking, hanging pictures, staring at these walls. . . .

For years I've heard about the wrench writers suffer from a change in environment. Romantic nonsense, I thought: they move *because* they don't want to write. Not so, I find now. Even my hand is different in relation to this new space. And my mind is a different mind, already a different size and shape.

I am in what would be the living room, if this apartment were being used residentially. It is a big room, a room in which to write *Fat*. Beryl's room is what would be the bedroom, three times larger than where she worked before, a room in which to type *Fat*. The kitchen is filled with stationery and files; it is a room to supply *Fat*. I feel all this. My ambitions swell. How can I whisper? I am almost forced to shout from room to room. "Beryl, comfort me," I could scream.

"Comfort *me*. I'm in the bedroom," her voice, in my mind, screams back.

This apartment, though new, is filled with echoes and ghosts. . . .

The air-conditioning purrs. The lights hum. The acoustic tile and carpeting absorb me. I am lost in all this space and texture. It is taking me a while to find myself. Perhaps I am where I was in business. Perhaps I'll go back to writing nights and weekends.

But meanwhile I have been arranging the books in my office. That means dusting them, putting them in alphabetical order, skimming or reading or re-reading many before I place them on the new shelves in my office/studio/living room. Yes, I've obliged my wife, I've taken every book out of the library. Now she can do what she wants with that room. I've got this one.

It's hard to figure out why I saved some of these books, what was in my mind, what was in the minds of their authors. A move is a time for housecleaning, mindcleaning. Though moved here, I put less than half the books on the shelves. The rest will go to some worthy cause, some institutional library— the children's school, a hospital, the armed services, the merchant marine—a project for Beryl while she paces *her* office, getting used to *her* space, and waiting for a word from me.

Poor Beryl. Even the bills have slowed down—I've had no time to shop. I've had time to do *nothing*.

hers: #12

I don't like it. The house is empty. There's only me, the phone, an occasional delivery, and Ruby. I can't talk to her for long. Talking while we cook is enough.

Even when there was a wall between me and my husband, at least I knew he was here, behind it. Now several buildings separate us.

It was different, years ago, when he went to business. At the beginning in our tiny apartment, we spent most nights making love, and I slept a good part of the day. There was hardly any shopping to do, hardly any phone calls to make—we had no "social life." In our next apartment, in that larger space, I learned—I had to learn—to cook and drink and use the phone. Then came our son, our house, our daughter, in that order. For a while, both children were home during the day, then one, then none. Is it any wonder I encouraged my husband to leave business and welcomed him home?

The wonder is that he thinks otherwise. He insists that he—he alone—made the decision to leave and that I never accepted his being here, him or his secretary. True, at first I made mistakes. I would go into his office to tell him about some delivery on Ruby's day off or something in the house that needed fixing. He taught me to knock before entering. But that turned out not to be the issue.

"Would you ask me to do these things if I were still in business?" he'd ask in that rhetorical style of his. "No, you had more respect for my work then. You wouldn't have barged into a conference, and you can't accept that I'm in conference now—with myself. . . . You didn't know what I was doing then, but you assumed it was important. Now I show you my work, and you disparage it."

In business he became accustomed to daily approbative response. He needs it still, as he works alone (on *Fat*, or *Whispers* or whatever). That's one of the things which worries me about his having moved to that cold bare apartment, reminiscent of business, but with no one to talk to but her, *his* Ruby. Even Marx had the distraction of other researchers in that British Museum library, and he had Engels to talk to.

There were other mistakes. Perhaps I should have fussed more over his lunch, fussed invisibly, in accordance with his aristocratic ideal of silent invisible service. However, I was always torn between the fussing and the invisibility. On some days I simply forgot his lunch or got tied up on the phone. Several times when he came down to the dining room and his place wasn't set, he referred again to using the delicatessen. But I could never do that. There are always things in the refrigerator, things to use up; and besides delicatessens remind me too much of secretaries—the friends of lonely men, married and single.

I wonder what he eats now. Those delicatessen sandwiches, I'll bet. Something's making him lose weight. That thin machine-sliced meat or just pacing in his new large room or. . . . I wonder if he eats with Beryl.

I have suggested that he make more luncheon dates. He explains that they cut too deep into his day, that he must stop work by eleven or eleven-thirty to shave, shower, and dress. Dressing takes longer now than when he was in business—a suit's one thing; a sports ensemble is another.

I have a romantic idea: I will make lunch for him once a week, on Ruby's day off. We will have a martini or two, eat, and make love until the children return from school. I will send him an invitation—again, of course, marked PERSONAL. I will emphasize informal dress, no need to shave, the approximateness of the hour—he can work as late as he likes.

It is a week later. Our lunch went beautifully. Everything was out for the martinis—he didn't even have to ask for a lemon—and the platter of Scotch salmon was attractively presented with capers, toast, more lemon. The wine was cold. He was appreciative of the cocktails, the food, the wine, *me*. Between bites of salmon we kissed, and after lunch we ran upstairs. For that too I had prepared: blinds down, bedspread off, diaphragm in. A soft light leaked through the blinds.

"Do you miss me?" I asked.

"Not now."

"But when you're down the block?"

"Of course."

"Not 'of course.' Say it."

"I'll write you another concrete poem: I miss you, I miss you, I miss you, I miss. . ."

"*I miss you.*"

Later he said, "D'you know who I don't miss? Beryl." The way he said that, gently and playfully, I knew what it must be like to be talked to as a mistress. I hope he never says things to her about me. Bad enough he writes.

Several more weeks have gone by. Why be so vague? I know the exact number. Four—we've had four more lunches, four more matinees. Ruby's day off has become my favorite day of the week—and his too, I think. Last time he shaved.

I wonder how Beryl's taking all this. She can type his whispers, but I'm *receiving* them . . . in the ear . . . in the cunt . . . I was right not to move to a larger house or apartment. Things have a way of working out—or *in*. I can hardly write a word these days without feeling its sexual connotation. For me, as for my husband, there was a period when I thought about sex *all the time*. Not in his terms—I saw no pubic grass, no breasts in the sky, no lips (falling perhaps like leaves), no sexual landscapes or city scapes—but *in me* I felt spring thaw, rivers rise, fish moving upstream. Then came the children, the house (houses now), the cooking, the drinking. . . . It's only recently I've begun to feel my juices run again, freely and intensely. It's as though we've been on separate vacations: him at business, *mon homme des affaires*, and me at home, *la dame de la maison*. The reunion was difficult—it has taken years—but I insist that things are working out *and in*.

There are other changes: I'm coming down to breakfast earlier now—partly to see the children before they go off to school, but mostly to see *him*. The children leave—our daughter still called for by private bus, our son walking to the subway. There are goodbye shouts. Sometimes my husband leaves with the children (he says that's his best hour, the one before Beryl arrives: another lovely sign). Sometimes he continues to read the papers, his papers, the *Times* and *Wall Street Journal*. I read my *Women's Wear Daily*. Ruby, in the kitchen, reads the *News*.

Those last three statements seem so simple, and yet they represent more than twenty years of marital adjustment. I remember how, at first, we used to bicker over the *Times*. Then it was understood that he got the first section first. But gradually it became understood also that, if a story continued into the second section, he had the right to reclaim *that*. Finally it was understood that he read the whole paper first. Understood in *his* mind. Never in mine.

We tried other procedures. He would start with the second section. Inevitably there'd be some financial story that began in the first, and he'd want it back. We tried everything but buying two *Times*. He suggested that. I thought it wasteful and refused. Besides, twin papers, like twin beds, indicate a bad marriage. Give me a double bed, even if the blankets are sometimes pulled away.

Perhaps the *Times* was responsible for his getting up early and my sleeping late. Now, more than twenty years later, the only reminder of all this is on Sundays. Then there's no *W.W.D.* for me, no *W.S.J.* for him. (There is a *News* for Ruby.) He and I grab the obvious sections, race through them, and fight for the hard news. . . . Another game. Object: to see how fast he can get through the entire paper. One Sunday when he got up early and I wasn't there clutching the Magazine Section, he made it in 27 minutes. I don't mean he read every word—I guess that would take all week—but he read more than just what interested him. I tested him, not only on moves made by The Department of the Treasury and by various chess players in the midst of a tournament—I knew he would score well on these—but moves made by politicians, student radicals, ballplayers, astronauts. . . His mind absorbs facts, while mine bogs down in feelings. Maybe that's why he reads faster.

Enough. Everyone knows about breakfast and newspapers. I have other things to do. I'm redecorating the library. Soon I'll begin working on other rooms. My husband will like that, all the buying and selling. Yes.

his: #13

"...ugh...ich...hm...oh..."

I'm not sure the subject of newspapers is exhausted. These are the sounds my wife makes as she reads the *W.W.D.*, the same sounds she used to make when she read the first or second section of the *Times*. Even then there were openings ("ugh"), happenings ("ich"), events ("hm"), parties ("oh") to which we were not invited—or to which we were. Echoes of yesteryear, but still... But still today.

I read silently, if not in silence—and perhaps, as she says, moving my lips. However, the ughing and iching goes on in my mind. Each day I look for me in the papers, a habit acquired in busines; but now I am never there. There are none of those small promotions which the company's publicity department handled so well, no photographs of myself staring at me from the financial page, no descriptions of myself as "spokesman for the company" or "its representative" at some meeting of some trade association. I no longer exist in the *Times*. I even look for myself on the obituary page. I don't exist there either. I don't exist, dead or alive. The paper seems designed, edited only to tell me *that*, what the world has been telling me since I left business. One day, I'm sure, I'll open the paper and see a review of *Fat*, my permission to exist again. Then I suppose the editors will have to scurry through their dead files and morgues and rag-paper editions and microfilms, inserting items about me; because if the book exists,

I must have existed, I must have been doing something.

Or perhaps a review of *Whispers*, that collaboration proving that I didn't exist alone, that my wife and I were alone together. Or *The Complete Correspondence*. Or *The Notebooks*. Yes, some morning, some series of mornings, the *Times* will surprise me. It will admit I exist.

his: #14

I know I was going to go on to describe an aristocrat who every morning had his butler iron the *Times*—his *Times*, the London *Times*—because the crease crossing the page irritated him. He didn't like to see the world divided so blatantly between those who rise above and those who fall below the fold... Yes, for me, unlike my wife, the subject of newspapers is endless; all subjects are; and all endings, arbitrary. I will let my thirteenth whisper stop where it does, chopped short there by a knife, my knife, as arbitrary as his butler pressing his *Times*, as arbitrary as life itself. I no longer look for order, except in the obituary columns.

The fact is I've been too busy to add to my thirteenth whisper. I've been adding instead to *Fat*, at the rate of about 600 words per day, and I realize that that book, that peculiar counter-revolutionary thesis, could also go on forever. Money, like newspapers, is not a subject that can be easily exhausted. No *enoughs* for me. My wife is right—I ask for *more*. Knowing that—that *Fat* will continue to grow and that I am becoming impatient—I have given an agent the first 217 pages (another arbitrary swipe of the esthetic knife).

"Place this," I pled in a whisper, thinking it shouldn't be hard—everyone's interested in money.

I waited more than a month, another 20,000 words, before phoning the agent.

"We don't call clients about rejections," he informed me.

"But not knowing is as much of a distraction as any rejection."

"You must learn to accept rejection."

I didn't like the way he said it, but he was right. Copies of the first few chapters of *Fat* had gone, in pieces, to several magazines; the 217 pages, in their arbitrary entirety, to three book publishers. No one was interested. Not anybody. That was the shocker, the possibility that maybe I would never read that review in the *Times*, that maybe after all the *Times* is right, that maybe I no longer exist.

I let over two months pass before calling the agent again. He took three days to return my call, but still I tried to be casual:

"I'll be going out of town for the summer. I was just wondering if anything has happened?"

"*Fat's* been circulating. Hunks of it have gone to more magazines, the whole beginning has gone to half a dozen book publishers. It's at another house now. I'll let you know if anything happens."

"I can give you another couple of hundred pages."

"What we've got is a fair sampling. If anyone wants more, I'll call you."

The summer is over. The call hasn't come. *Fat* is almost finished. I have no idea how many editors have rejected it. I keep telling myself that it doesn't matter, that my satisfaction must come from the work itself and not from the world's acceptance of it, that that's why I left business. I try not to think about how quickly my calls used to be returned, how much my work was appreciated, how many people wanted things from me. I tell myself that *Fat* is a good book, a substantial piece of work, that the rejections can't change the book itself, that many books (many less eccentric than *Fat*) have met with re-

sistence, have even had to be published privately. . . . I toy
with that idea, but my pride won't let me publish at my own
expense. My pride is too great for that and yet not great
enough to support rejections forever.

The rejections *are* important. They *do* matter. They seep
through my system and into my work. The work changes. It
becomes slightly bitter. Some days I find myself grinding out
my 600 words or so, mechanically and without joy. Or, like
now, I turn to these whispers for relief. Or I respond affirma-
tively to requests for my time on committees, in order to affirm
my existence in the world's eyes. I do what I can to keep on
writing. I whisper now, but can think of nothing but *Fat*, that
rejected hunk of myself.

hers: #13

Fat is finished. He handed me two thick black spring binders, each squeezing about five hundred typed pages. "Printed, it'll only be five or six hundred altogether," he said, as if assuring me that it was really a thin book, not yet reduced to anything like its ultimate skinniness; just something he had dashed off during the past five years or so, between letters, whispers, checks; a few pounds of typescript that he'd appreciate my glancing through and commenting on.

It's slow going. Especially difficult to read in the fragments of time I can steal during the day and after the children have gone to bed. But, I would guess, difficult even under the best conditions—what he would consider the best and I, the worst: some quiet reading room in which there's nothing to do but that, hour after hour, without relief.

What he calls his "bibliographical/anthological method" *is* difficult; elliptical. Between one book cited and the next, even between one quotation and the next from the same book, the distances are long and the connections complex. I cannot leap; I crawl, slowly digesting phrases like "Shit is an acquired taste" (ugh), slowly following his General Laws of Compensation (ich) and his arguments against dialectical materialism (hm). In *Fat* there are no conflicts between classes. All classes are ideally married. They exist only to serve each other, to produce and consume. Perhaps *Fat* itself is an example of the process it describes: his mysterious accretive production, my slow fragmented consumption. It is difficult—the difficulties mount—for me to experience the book as anything but autobiography, the product of his years of business, retirement (as much now from home as from business), reading, marriage, children. . . just as I expect him to sit down to one of my dinner parties and understand that it is a product of *my* life, *my* business, *my* reading, *my* world of goods and services produced and distributed in this economic drama we share. When, in *Fat*, he mentions a servant, I know he means Ruby. When he mentions a secretary, he means Beryl. "Children" are *our* children. And so on, through doctors, lawyers, brokers, rental agents, antique dealers, TV repairmen, down to the bitsiest bit player in our economic play—each is ours, and we are theirs. Maybe he thinks he has written objective economic theory, discovered general laws. I know better. I recognize everyone in this fat book. I recognize the dominant theme of marriage. I recognize exchange rates, trade routes, negotiating positions, the language of love expressed in yen, francs, pesos, guilders, kroner, lire, pounds, dollars. . . *Fat* could not have been written by anyone but him, and he couldn't have written it without me. It is *our* book—it practically says that, right at the beginning, on the dedicatory page.

I progress slowly, skimming nothing, not one quotation, not one footnote. I read every word, every letter of every word. I delight in correcting an occasional typo or misspelling. She, that other collaborator of his, that mechanical collaborator is not as perfect as he thinks. I wonder if she even understands what she types: this golden song dedicated to me, to our marriage; this longest letter I've ever received. Does she know that it was written in isolation (even if in proximity to her), because that way he appreciates me most intensely, that way I am there without talking, while she pounds the keys of her machine in that ex-bedroom?

I have been averaging fifty pages a day and yet, no matter what my rate, it is not fast enough for him. Each time we meet—at breakfast, if I'm down early; on Ruby's day off; evenings; in bed—he looks at me peculiarly, expectantly. He never asks how I'm doing, how I'm enjoying it—he waits. These days (over two weeks now) I think he resents my reading anything but *Fat*. He scowls as I make my noises over *W.W.D.* I wonder what he'd think if he heard me making the same sounds over *Fat*. Would he know that I'm expressing pleasure? Pleasure *and pain*—difficulty, I've been calling it. Reading *Fat* is like delivering a child, *our* child. I cannot separate it from its parents. I leave that to critics and psychiatrists.

This time I have made up my mind not to fall into the trap of playing critic. The book is what it is—him, me, us— I accept it as he would wish, without reservations, without buts. I even hesitate to make just one suggestion, about one small word: the title, that harsh misleading monosyllabic *Fat*. I'd rather see the book called almost anything else; but preferably some catchy phrase that suggests the subject. For example, I've thought of *It's Only Money*. People would buy that. They don't want one-word titles—there's nothing to hang onto, and *Fat's* more slippery, more elusive than most.

As I finish reading the book, I see there is only one paragraph (way back in the introduction) that would have to be cut in order to change the title:

> *A wife observes that* fat *would be a better word for* money *than* bread. *She thinks of money as something extra, excessive, something one uses after all the necessities have been paid for by check or charge card. The idea of*

using money for anything but luxuries has hardly oc-curred to her.

Well, I am "a wife"—cutting that paragraph would af-fect me more than him. Initially, anyway. Ultimately, of course, we'd both benefit. The book would sell. It's strange that a man could spend so much time writing a book, without apparently giving much thought to the title. If I wrote one—all by myself, without his help—I'd spend more time on the title than anything else. Actually, I'd rather write titles than books.

his: #15

For years she has been saying, "Let's have some people over tonight." Or ". . . tomorrow." Or ". . . this weekend." It doesn't really matter when. And it doesn't matter who. What matters is the abstraction: *some people,* to fill some space/ time, to eat some food, to drink some drinks, to speak some words and hear some.

Now she says, "Let's go someplace." She means on vacation. Again it's that abstract. She doesn't care where, but perhaps the farther away, the better. She says she is exhausted and needs a change, a real change, not just a summer in the country. She never says exactly what has exhausted her, but I'm led to believe, by her hints and whispers, that it's *Fat,* that effort, sustained over so many years and culminating in reading it, making corrections, suggesting a catchier title (rejected by me—"Fat will be fashionable," I reply, quoting myself).

She marshals arguments for going someplace: *"Fat—"* she chokes on the word, spits it out with resignation—*"Fat* is being sent around by your agent. There's nothing you can do to help. Even when part of the book was being offered—" and rejected, she tactfully avoids saying—"you became increasingly irritable."

This argument is strong. I am becoming not only irritable but distracted from doing other work, starting my next project. Every time the phone rings I expect it to be the agent. It never is. Perhaps he is right to call only about acceptance, but, as

I've told him, not knowing is unbearable, more distracting in some ways than rejection. Rejections are manageable. Like garbage, they can be disposed of. Or they can be rationalized away. It doesn't take long to invent a stupid editor or an insensitive publisher. But nothing, no word, silence is more difficult to dismiss. And the publishers have taken a vow of silence.

I spend hours dreaming about my first reader in some gigantic publishing house or communications conglomerate. She is a bright college girl, with intelligent eyes behind rosy Ben Franklin glasses, and pale make-up on her lips. She moistens them with her tongue as she reads. More and more quickly it darts in and out as she becomes caught up in the rhythm of my prose. She licks the words off the page. Her thighs become moist with joy. She cannot leave *Fat* at the office. Holding it tenderly to her bosom, she takes it home. There, having broken her date for the evening, she reads it in bed, fingering herself for relief from the excitement of my words, shimmering, dazzling, glistening, tinkling, crackling on the page. She had never realized that money could be so thrilling a subject... This revelation is there, the next morning, in her report urging immediate publication.

The second reader, an associate editor, is even more impressed than the first. He has read her report—rather too superlative, too ecstatic, too general—and discounted it as the gushing hysteria of a schoolgirl. But now he reads *Fat* and is forced to admit his prejudice. He sustains an erection throughout its thousand typed pages. His report is more detailed and specific than the girl's. He likes the way the author has presented the history of money as a movement from the bartering of necessities to the buying of luxuries and leisure. He likes "fat" as what he calls a "controling metaphor." He likes the use of the Bible and Shakespeare and popular songs. He likes the General Laws of Compensation. He likes everything. PUBLISH THIS, his lengthy memorandum shrieks more loudly than the girl's.

The editor-in-chief doesn't have to be persuaded. He is seasoned and discerning. He reads the reports. He hardly has to read the book. After so many years at his job, he is able to focus on that one word or phrase which illuminates a page. For him books are only brief passages that other readers might underline. In the whole history of prose literature there are just a few sentences which he would mark and save in their entirety; and no complete paragraphs, none—not one by anyone—that would not benefit by his editing. However, he is a practical man. He accepts the rest—all those other thousands and millions of words—as packaging, as oysters that are necessary to produce the pearls. I understand. When I was in business there were all those hours between the brief moments when a contract was signed.

He finds enough bright spots on my pages—between all that dark ink, all that mourning ribbon—to justify a strong recommendation to the publisher. I imagine his report, his memo, experienced and forceful, ending: . . . *This is a book we should buy. It will sell.* In my mind I read it as a telegram: IT WILL SELL STOP (*Fat* will sell as well as *It's Only Money.* Yes.)

I see his secretary, his Beryl, his one-in-a-million, handing the memo to the publisher's secretary, *his* Beryl. The wheels begin to turn faster. My mind races. Yes, the publisher says, based on the editor-in-chief's synopsis. Yes, yes, yes. He calls a special meeting of the board, gathers his captains about him—his banker, his lawyer, his accountant, his manufacturer of typeface, his producer of ink, his printer, his binder, the

ancient director whose grandfather founded the firm. . . I see
them seated around the boardroom table, each with badges of
gray or white at his temples, each with a hard cool no-nonsense
look in his eyes (including the glass eye of the founder's
grandson) . . . These are not men who waste their time reading
books; they buy and sell them.

The publisher-chairman proposes a $100,000 advertising
budget for *Fat*. "Do I hear a second?"

(A second $100,000? I wonder.)

"Second."

"Proposed and seconded. All in favor?"

A collective aye. (A collective eye, a collective ear.)

"Opposed?"

(Silence.)

The motion is passed.

My fantasy does not stop here. I'm already sketching the
jacket cover, and writing the blurb and the hard-sell endorse-
ments by writers who have been given advance copies, and the
ads which will move the book out into the world. I hold a pen
or pencil in every hand. I am an octopus. . . I go to the john
between my office and Beryl's and look in the mirror. What I
see will never sell books. Not that blank gray octopus face. . .
There will be no dustjacket photo, but more words. . . I pick
up another pen in another hand. I struggle to interpret and
present the author's intentions. I identify with my editors and
have increased respect for them. They are heroic. They at-
tempt the impossible. No wonder newspaper reviewers lean
on them, quote from their blurbs. I would too. I pick up still
another pen in still another hand. My reviews of me are
extravagant.

There is a final fantasy—one which intrudes, against my
wishes. In it, once again I see that college girl. . . . Now her

back is to me. Her hair falls softly on her broad shapely shoulders. Her puckered elbows are braced on the arms of her posture chair. She is obviously holding a heavy book. I look past her at the manuscripts stacked against the wall in front of her desk. There, at the bottom of the pile, beneath all the other claimants for her attention, is *Fat.* . . . Her phone rings. It's her boyfriend. He has to make one midtown call, then he's free for the rest of the day. Can she take off? Meet him at his apartment? Or hers? "Yes," she sings, leaning forward in a lovely arc of vertebrae, and caressing the phone, "anywhere, anytime—there's nothing holding me."

But maybe that last was not a fantasy. . . Anyway, my wife was supposed to be marshaling arguments, not me marshaling fantasies (which is itself a fantasy—at best I marshal words, get them moving, galloping only when I'm very lucky) . . . .

Her penultimate argument is brief: she reminds me that this is the first summer both children will be at camp, a perfect time for us to go someplace. Her ultimate argument is brief too: it is important for me to visit foreign markets, to keep in touch.

She is through. Her arguments are marshaled, waiting at some pier or airport to be shipped overseas. I am persuaded by everything she has said—except the basic thing, the need for a vacation. I resent the suggestion more than when I was in business, because now I am doing more exactly what I want, even if my efficiency in getting my product out into the world is not as great as it was then. Now the suggestion of a vacation does not seem intended to slow me down, but to stop me altogether. Why now should I be drafted as a tourist? Manipulated by marital management? Monopolized by my wife?

What have I done wrong? Written a book that has not been immediately accepted? Is that all? Or am I being punished for leaving business? . . . Why can't I spend another summer at our country place? There, I write mornings, mail my stuff to Beryl in the city, swim or play tennis or sail in the afternoon, drink from six on, return the sun I absorb during the day to my wife at night (in strong healthy bursts). There, there's *continuity*.

I use that word and discover it's exactly what my wife doesn't want. Again she says that she wants *a change* and— and, more explicitly now—that she is exhausted from the effort of collaborating on *Fat*. It was different when I was in business, she says. Then she knew even less about what I was doing; then she didn't have to support the strain; then she was younger. . . She is exhausted, she repeats; she needs refreshment, replenishment—again, in short, *a change*.

I don't get the full impact of this phrase until, in an effort to compromise, I suggest a quick trip to Spain. Once again, over martinis, as I open the atlas volume of the encyclopaedia, I think I see blue-gray Spain in her blue-gray eyes. But no, that isn't what she wants either. Spain is another lump of continuity, a fist clenching Portugal like bright brass knuckles. No, she wants to explore new markets. She wants *me* to explore new markets. She won't play the color-game. Instead she plays a time-game. The long nail of her index finger quickly traces a triangular trip from London to Amsterdam to Paris. She proposes about a week in each. This way we'll qualify for the 21-day excursion rate. She suggests dates of departure and return, so our anniversary will come in Paris and so we'll still be back in time for the children's visiting day at camp. Everything falls into place. She marshals time as efficiently as arguments. She is happy. She has a project. She rushes dinner so she can get upstairs and begin to pack.

Her happiness makes me happy. I try not to remember what it's like traveling: that 24-hours-a-day test of marriage: packing and unpacking, moving from hotel to hotel, meal to meal, drink to drink, entertainment to entertainment, shop to shop, museum to museum, cathedral to cathedral . . . avoiding tours to create our own . . . moving, no matter in what direction, always toward home . . . comparing always with home . . . her guilt about the children, mine about work . . . all to convince ourselves, so strenuously, that we no longer need a change, that we've had a vacation, that exhaustion is relative.

Beryl and I do what we can to smooth the way. We arrange for the most direct flights at the most convenient hours; reserve the most comfortable rooms in the most elegant hotels; renew passports; get vaccination certificates; buy traveler's checks, pounds, guilders, francs; read foreign publications to see what events to get tickets for. . . I dictate letters to friends in Europe, preparing them for our arrival, and to bankers, lawyers, and stockbrokers here, advising them of our departure. I spread our itinerary around—even send one to my agent, just in case.

In my mind (again, always), I am paged at the Ritz bar, when the telegram arrives. I hand *le gargon* the appropriate tip, open the envelope, and read the tardy, but inevitable, message: FAT ACCEPTED STOP FIFTY THOUSAND ADVANCE AGAINST STANDARD ROYALTIES STOP YOU RETAIN SUBSIDIARY RIGHTS STOP HOLLYWOOD INTERESTED STOP. I reread this poem, committing it to memory, and for the second time enjoying its modernity, the rushing rhythm punctuated only by breaths, the unmodified verbs. . . .

"Is everything all right?" my wife asks.

I take another sip of martini and, without comment, without the slightest trace of surprise, I hand her the telegram. Now she reads it, rereads it, smiles, hesitates. . . "It's not a joke is it? Something *you* wrote? It's—*real?*"

"I assume it is."

"WOW!" She wobbles on the barstool, can hardly keep her balance. Her book has been accepted. "Let's fuck," she whispers in my ear.

All the preparations are made. For three weeks, in that abstract world of tourism, I know exactly where I'll be—my itinerary tells me—something I never know in the freer, more improvised, more accident-prone world of writing. The vacation will be like a brief return to business. Not only will I know where I'm going, I will feel useful. Already, I feel useful. I'm spending money faster than usual. Bills pour in for airline tickets, matched luggage bought by my wife, and dresses that pack better than what she wears here. . . . The trip is becoming a reality, if just the overture to what she'll buy in Paris, what I'll buy in London (well, maybe only accessories—there'll be no time to have suits properly fitted) . . . . Charges are made to my checking account for the traveler's checks, the foreign money. . . . The bank is busy, I am busy, Beryl is busy. My wife's enthusiasm is catching. There is hardly time anymore to think of *Fat*—it is now only a dull pain in the back of my head.

Beryl makes up lists and schedules. Shopping lists. Doctor lists. Cleaning schedules. Camp schedules. While we are gone she will play mistress to Ruby, mother to the children. She will call them at camp and report to us in London, Amsterdam, Paris. . . . But now the limousine she has ordered is here. The separate, neatly designated envelopes containing tickets, passports, health certificates, hotel confirmations, traveler's checks, foreign currency are packed flat at the top of my overnight bag (three weeks of overnights!). We are off, on vacation, going someplace.

his: #16

We're back.

Anticipation of the trip was the basic experience, not the trip itself. We jumped from the future into the past, barely touching the present. It exists in a few journal entries. I give these to my wife.

hers: #14

Yes, we're back. Back from Europe. Back from visiting the children at camp. Back from six weeks in the country (two with the children when they returned from camp). I don't know where the summer has gone. The children are at school again. My husband is in that apartment with Beryl. There's no word on *Fat*. We're seeing the psychiatrist twice a week. It's fall rather than spring. Otherwise everything's about the same.

About the same. . . My husband was right—the change changed nothing. Not for me, anyway. And the other changes are miniscule:

The children lost a few pounds and gained a few inches. They ran us ragged on visiting day, competing for our attention, pulling us in opposite directions from activity to activity (our daughter's volleyball, our son's baseball; her nature walks, his woodcraft), until finally we were seated together in the "recreation building" listening to songs and watching skits. Pop, the camp director, beamed. Parents' cameras flashed. There was no smoking. My husband chewed pine needles. . . .When it was time to leave, the children ran to the messhall, laughing—even my daughter, away from home for the first time!

From that long long visiting day only a single scrap of dialogue lingers.

A friend of my daughter's asked her: "Is that your father?"

"Yes."

"Is he nice?"

"Yes."

"Does he scream?"

"No."

"That's nice."

Ruby was irritable after our trip. She said Beryl had been bossy, and she muttered something about movin' on. My husband suggested giving her a raise, making that compensatory gesture. I did, and she's cheerful again.

Of course, Ruby's raise meant increases (quarterly and annual) in social security and unemployment insurance, a recomputation of tax rate . . . all work for Beryl, leading to a raise for her too. God knows what she gets now—for doing half the work Ruby does. Whatever the amount, she seems unusually happy. Her voice bubbles on the phone when she calls to check on a bill or to give me a message from my husband. If I didn't know she was such a confirmed spinster, I'd think a man had come into her life. Something has happened. Maybe, if it's not a man and not the raise, she has inherited money.

And my husband? Are there any changes, however miniscule, in him? Just one. He has started a new book. Or, perhaps more accurately, the same book, with a new title. This one he calls tentatively *Flea Markets*. (He does come up with the most unappetizing titles.) I saw the book emerging (re-emerging) in each city we visited. In London, as in the others, he saw the people he really wanted to—the lecturers in economics at the universities, writers on the staffs of important financial journals, government officials—and he did his shopping. His shopping for the things he wanted. Only then was he willing to shop with me, to shop just to shop, in the abstract, for nothing in particular.

I led him one Saturday to the flea market on Portobello Road. As soon as we were there I knew he was hooked. All through the morning, walking up and down the steep crowded street, stopping at stalls and going into shops, he was writing, making notes on the back of receipts, ticket stubs, matchbook covers, anything he had in his pockets. While I bought a powder horn for our son and a heart-shaped Victorian pincushion for our daughter, he wrote. He could hardly wait to return to the hotel and get at some decent stationery. And that night over drinks he was still scribbling—on the cocktail napkins.

At this flea market—and subsequently at those in Amsterdam and Paris—he hardly spoke. He said something once about these markets being a microcosm and then: "You move through them so easily, the way you do through a supermarket at home... All these lives, stretched out on the ground, and in wagons, and on racks... Don't you feel sad?" I had to admit that I didn't, that I was too busy shopping.

I remember some of his jottings, each scrap dated, and arranged now by Beryl on neatly typed chronological sheets in his notebook. I miss the random documentary feel of his original notes and the variation in handwriting adapted to different-sized scraps. I refer now to the notebook only to get his words right. Everything else is wrong. It's dismaying to think that someday this notebook may be published, PRINTED, completely ruined. Anyway:

The refuse of the world, the refused rejected things of refused rejected people.

The meaning and meaninglessness of endless rows of clothes, books, bottles, jewelry, furniture . . . all these things which once meant something to someone, things for which people traded their lives.

> *Repeated ugliness, repeated beauty: the beauty cre-*
> *ated by repetition. (Consider Pollock, Ossorio, Arman,*
> *Warhol, serial painters, Color Field. . . Consider every*
> *artist who ever lived and created his own flea market.)*
> *The beauty—and horror of endlessness, of infinity.*

> *The continuous circle of objects moving from hand*
> *to hand, life to life, home to home. Second-hand is an*
> *understatement. Infinity-hand. Hundreds of empty*
> *gloves. . . .*

> *The natural artless order of confusion. The ten-*
> *dency to classify by types and thereby to neutralize ob-*
> *jects. What is unique stands out like a work of art and*
> *is, typically, like such a work, useless. The choice be-*
> *tween anonymous things we need and distinctive things*
> *we don't need (sometimes called art, sometimes bric-a-*
> *brac).*

> *My wife finds none of this sad. Perhaps I do because*
> *I no longer want anything. I feel old remembering a time*
> *when there were things I wanted—and old seeing what*
> *happens to those things. Despite advertisements to the*
> *contrary, there is* nothing *for the man who has every-*
> *thing.*

I was beginning to think we had spent our entire trip in flea markets, but here's a clipping from the *Sunday Times* (London) which deals presumably with another world. The thing itself, the actual clipping is this time scotch-taped onto the notebook page, prompted no doubt by Beryl's laziness and not by sensitivity:

> *The statutes under which pros-*
> *ecutions can be brought against*

> *publishers, booksellers and paper*
> *and magazine vendors include the*
> *Vagrancy Act, which was enacted*
> *in 1824 to stop soldiers returning*
> *from the Napoleonic Wars exhib-*
> *iting their wounds and begging.*

Down the margin he scribbled:

> *Yes, let's*
> *stop writers*
> *and artists*
> *from exhibiting*
> *their wounds.*
> *But why*
> *soldiers?*

And there are other reminders (once again typed) of worlds beyond flea markets—or reminders, anyway, that we had to get from one flea market to the next—his hurried thoughts which will, I suppose, eventually be spun out into long paragraphs . . . pages . . . chapters . . . books . . . *the book,* containing all the obsessive fragments. . . *The Complete Works:*

> *Caricature is the art of speed, what we see when travel-*
> *ing fast.*

> *Next year my wife and I will go to the moon. The ulti-*
> *mate "travel package": to be opened on delivery. The*
> *destination becomes an end in itself, superseding the*
> *trip.*

> *There is no escape from escape.*

> *Travel conventions are similar to psychiatric conven-*
> *tions. It's not enough to dredge up anxieties, one must*
> *pay for them. In travel we deal with dozens of doctors*

*masquerading as cab drivers, porters, stewards, and stew-
ardesses, pilots and co-pilots, innkeepers, desk clerks,
bartenders, waiters, bellboys, maids, elevator operators,
customs inspectors, police...*

The basic business machine is the clock.

Art doesn't last, we learn in business.

*On vacation we don't even have weekends to look for-
ward to. It's all weekends, a seemingly endless void of
weekends.... I sympathize with artists. They're on vaca-
tion all the time.*

*We should have mercenaries take vacations for us.
Artists.*

*My wife hears a child crying and responds as if it were
one of ours. I remind her that ours are at camp... And
yet when we hear children crying in Europe, they are al-
most always the children of tourists. They cry for their
parents.*

The ideal, as in chess: to be mobile and *protected.*
Then back to the flea markets, without, so typically, a clue
that we had fun playing the same games as at home, that they
were even intensified by travel:

*Paris, particularly, makes me feel old with its em-
phasis on eating. It's one big restaurant. I wish I had
the appetite I once had. I taste. My wife finishes what's
left on my plate. She says she's can't bear waste.*

*My theme: the omnipresence of waste. Hers: saving
things from oblivion.*

Old age is waste, second-hand things, flea markets...

It is our anniversary. I see kids kissing in the street and along the parapets of these beautiful Paris bridges. I think of kissing my wife, here in the open, but to do so at our age would be grotesque. Old kisses belong in the flea market, lined up in row after row, among all the hundreds and thousands of other kisses that have become worthless anonymous bargains. . .

Back also to *Flea Markets,* the book, the things one finds *there,* the things perhaps that couldn't fit in *Fat,* the things abandoned by *Fat* to emerge now again, arranged neatly, maybe too neatly, by Beryl:

Property is an extension of the self.

Thoreau's epitaph might be: He lived close to the bone. And mine: He lived close to the fat.

And then two midget whispers—maybe only murmurs, or poems (let out of their customary stockades and set free on the page, like those tender shrunken *haiku* of so long ago):

1) *Like casualties in war
   in business dollars
   are the way
   of keeping score.*

2) *Early each morning
   I start my work.
   By noon I begin
   to sip my reward.*

The second of these is followed by this note:

Enjambment! For me this technical term has industrial magic. I imagine a logjam at a paper mill. And yet the term means just the opposite of a businessman's block. It suggests the easy flow, the continuation of a poet's ideas and feelings from the end of one line to the begin-ning of the next.

Then, on a fresh page, there are four entries:

This journal, this reliquary containing a few hairs and fingernail parings—or bitings. . .

Malaise! Isn't there an English word for it? An Ameri-can word? A New York word?

In business the problem is tension.
In art the problem is anxiety.
In business I felt the problem in my gut.
Now, in writing, I feel it everywhere.
In business I felt it mostly at the end of the day.
Now I feel it all the time.
Both business and writing have their own ways of mak-ing me feel alive.
Travel reminds me that I have a life somewhere else.

The world doesn't necessarily reward one for what he does best but for what it wants most. One is very lucky if what he does best is what the world wants. More often the world tries to persuade one that what it wants is what one does best.
One is me.

There the trip ends—the trip, loosely defined as a busi-ness trip. With a quotation from Lytton Strachey's "The End of General Gordon," the journal resumes a tone that is schol-arly. Of Tien Wang of Nankin Strachey writes:

"In the recesses of his seraglio, the Celestial King, judging that the time had come for the conclusion of his mission, swallowed gold leaf until he ascended to Heaven."

The next entry is from the New York *Times,* another clip-
ping—something about "noise pollution"—the actual clip-
ping again, more of Beryl's laziness, but real. . . communal
flesh. . . . And then this scrap of homecoming dialogue:

*Daughter: "You're lucky, you don't have to do anything,
you don't even have to go to school."*
*Father: "I have to do certain things, but they're dictated
by me."*
Daughter: "That's what I mean. You don't really *have to
do anything."*
Father: "You're beginning to sound like your mother."

And finally, after so many pages, so many years, so many
trys, a real honest-to-God seventeen syllable haiku, so appro-
priately culminating his work to date:

Nature has been raped
For haiku syllables
I must search my fat mind.

wHISpers
wHispERS
wHISpers
wHispERS
wHISpers
wHispERS
wHISpers
wHispERS
wHISpers
wHispERS
wHISpers
wHispERS
wHISpers
wHispERS
wHISpers
wHispERS
wHISpers
wHispERS
wHISpers
wHispERS
wHISpers
wHispERS
wHISpers
wHispERS
wHISpers

Part Four
(the present)

mine: #1

Are you disappointed? Did you want *more?* More of her criticism of me? More of her criticism of him? More of his of her? More of both of theirs of themselves? Of life? . . . Did you think they would go on whispering forever, until the day they died? Did you want *those* speeches, the essence of their lives, delivered from deathbeds in thin squeaky voices?

I'm sorry. I would have given you all that, but I only take dictation. I accept what's given to me. Like her, I accept endings; like him, I know there are none. Like her, I can't bear waste; like him, I know there is none, that everything is re-used, re-made, re-sold. . . Like her, like him—that's the point; they're both parts of me, two major fragments in a collection of fragments, these voices I hear in my head and record on paper.

I don't know what to call what I've written. Is it fiction, a novel—this rearrangement of my experience? Is that all there is to it—recording the voices one hears out there in the world and within one's own head, organizing scraps? The line between private and public is thin as a crease in the brain. Find the line, if you can, between fiction and non-fiction, autobiography and biography, poetry and prose. To avoid that impossible search we invent new labels: the non-fiction novel, the interpretive biography, the prose poem. . . so many pretty shades of gray. . . like the suits he used to wear. . .

I started college and liked literature. But they never told us the truth; never told us that there are no rules, that we are our rules; never told us about these voices we hear. They taught as though each writer had just one voice, one recognizable style, that single answer to a multiple choice, that blank to be filled in. If only they had explained that the one voice is collective . . . many voices . . . obsessions . . . ghosts, haunting us now, but existing in the past and future too. They didn't teach us about collaboration, only imagination. Even Shakespeare, Sweet William, was one voice, one consistent mellifluous voice. When a character of his was jealous, that was his imagination at work. When a character was ambitious, that was his imagination. When one was ambivalent or bawdy or "masculinely mad" or "femininely hysterical," these too were acts of imagination. When one thought of money. . . There was no clue that he *listened*, no clue that he *really* talked to ghosts.

If I don't know what category in which to place this book, you can guess how much harder is the more specific problem of a title. And she, my female character, thinks she would like *just* to write titles! Should I let her have her way, the first word as, in the book itself, I let her have—or, at least, record—the last? Should I call this *It's Only Money?* Or should I please him and call it *Fat* or *Flea Markets?* Or should I let an editor decide? I rather like the idea of further collaboration.

The ghosts which haunt my characters haunt me. When I had him caring so much about whether or not *Fat* would be published, I was caring about this book, the book you hold, having shown pieces to editors. And I suppose if this were what we are taught is a novel, if it had a plot as well as characters and setting, that that would be an "obligatory scene," a chapter: "The Acceptance of *Fat*." Or: "The Final Rejection of *Fat*." I can, of course, assure you now that *Fat* would eventually have been accepted—and, later, *Flea Markets* too. But I'm not that interested in obligatory scenes—peripheral scenes interest me more, the domesticated details of life, whispers. At times, like him, I want to eliminate the details (marriage, children, the need to earn a living). At other times, like her, I realize that these details are life itself.

Like him, I think I'm writing a book. Like her, I know I'm collaborating. . . .Like him, I see the meal on the table. Like her, I don't want you to think it just happened. . . He sees one continuous meal. She sees one continuous book. . . They're both right. . . .If the housewife is an artist, the artist is a housewife. . . . Like him, like her. . . .

The author must intrude, must break that rule too. You're entitled to know who's recording as well as who's speaking. Ask me anything, I'll hear your questions.

—Yes, I'm single, but not a "confirmed spinster." What an ugly phrase for her to have used. Perhaps I look older than I am. But still I want someday to marry and have children.

—No, I've never married. If, as you say, I seem so familiar with "the institution," it is again, because I've listened— and because, over the years, I've worked mostly for married men. I like them best. They're cool and efficient. At the office. And in bed. . . . Of course, this job has been different from the rest. I never worked in a man's home before. When he left business, none of the other girls wanted the job. They said they would go out of their minds, alone in a room with no one to talk to. There was that, which was always said first; and then, among the single girls, the reluctant admission that the chances of marriage would be reduced; and then—it sounds silly now, so many years later—but there *was* something stigmatic about working privately in a man's home—we knew the girls who worked as secretaries in hotels, knew the services *they* performed.

—I took the job because I knew there'd be more time for me to read and write. I welcomed the chance to know one man well, to see him at work *and* play. And I was curious to know how he'd spend his time, how he'd use his retirement. I had some abstract idea of retirement. I expected the bills, the solicitations, the routine correspondence, but not whispers, journal entries, *Fat, Flea Markets*, poems! . . . He gave me more than I bargained for. Sometimes he gave me more than his wife. There were even moments when I thought he'd leave her for me. I didn't listen carefully enough.

—Not until during those three weeks when they were on vacation. Then—with so few bills coming in, only occasional interruptions by Ruby, the weekly calls to their children at camp—only then did I begin really to listen and write.

—Of course, the dictation I took was not from them alone. I heard the voices of other men for whom I've worked and other wives I've known. I heard the voices of my parents and their friends. I heard my own voice as a child and as the spinster I'm determined not to become except by choice. . . . One listens, writes X words per day, and suddenly has a book. It's easy—if one is lonely enough and doesn't, like her, prefer the phone. . . At times, like her, I find a voice at the other end of the line. At times, like him, I write. . . That's one advantage Shakespeare had—there was no phone..

—Perhaps money does talk after all, if only to say hello. Perhaps that explains my interest in it. And his. And hers. . . . In "economic therapy," as he calls it, there's always someone to talk to—a salesman or saleslady, at least. . . Buying a suit

must be like buying another voice. . . . There are days when
even the typewriter repairman is a relief. . . Goods and serv-
ices *are* therapy. We stuff our mouths and ears with money,
dress our wounds, wear green bandages over our eyes. . . .
—I don't understand your question. Are you asking if
my book is about *the* urban experience? . . . It's about *mine.*
There must be many New Yorks. Mine is hard and tall. If it
exists, this city in my head, somewhere there must be a couple
living in it who speak with voices something like those I hear.
It can't be all imagined, any more than the purr of air-condi-
tioning, the hum of fluorescent lights, the suck of acoustic tile,
the crisp sounds of stationery being handled and pages
turned. . . .
—Like typewriter repairmen, books sometimes are a re-
lief when I'm alone. I listen to *their* authors listening to *their*
characters. I wonder how they separate the men from the
women—especially couples, where the voices grow together
and blend over the years, moving from poetry to prose. Some
ideas may typically be separable, but the voices? How does
one indicate pitch on the printed page? Must one use "he
said" and "she said," "he thought" and "she thought," like
silent musical notations, whispers within whispers, little whis-
pers, less than whispers, soundless words?
—Yes, since leaving college, having dropped in and out,
I'm self-taught: I just read and listen. . . No, I never even
went to secretarial school, just picked that up. . . No, I was
never tempted to work for a publishing house or an ad agency.
My friends did that, the ones who finished college, the ones
who got married. . . Oh, I see, you want some idea of my aca-
demic standing when I left. . . . Was I a good student? Did I
get good marks? My I.Q.? . . . I don't remember. B average,
I guess. I deserved A's in literature; I got B's. I deserved D's

in chemistry and things like that; I got B's. My I.Q., too, must
have been an approximation, I just don't remember. I don't
even remember if I took good notes at college or if that came
later. I think maybe during lectures I was knitting socks, lis-
tening to what the stitches told me. I never liked lectures—
they're too well organized.

—You think I've been hard on my characters, treated
them with a lack of tenderness? . . . There's no point in my
arguing with you. That's not my job. My job is to take dicta-
tion. I accepted my characters as I found them, heard them—
neither for better nor worse. . . . The man was under a strain
in business. He wanted to do something else. *I* let him, and *I*
let his wife let him. He hired me to help him through a transi-
tional period. I did what I was asked, made no demands on
him, and put no pressure on him to turn out more work (more
words). Men think women make demands, but men make
them upon themselves. She's right about that. . . And as for
her, I freed her from many of the details she had become
used to not bothering with during the years he was in business.
I gave her time for the other details she preferred. If she
hasn't whispered as many words as he, it's because she pre-
ferred to be doing something else. . . And what, after all,
have my characters done for me? He has expressed some ap-
preciation, some awareness of the things I do. But not without
reservation. And he has never really listened to me. And the
wife: she treats me like a bothersome piece of equipment.
There's none of the compassion she shows Ruby. At Christmas,
along with his bonus, there's her bottle of perfume and some
mechanical words. True, I may be more of a threat to her than
Ruby is, but I'm also more help. I've been holding their mar-
riage together, in my head, and on paper. That's part of a sec-
retary's job, a private secretary's. . . . If no man is a hero to

his valet, surely none is to his secretary. Nor is any man's wife.
—Yes, yes—my double positive—I like what I do. I like
the walk from subway to work. I like saying good morning now
to doorman and elevator operator. Especially when the morn-
ing isn't good, it's like having permission to lie. I like the ele-
vator's gentle ride better than those creaky stairs in that brown-
stone house. I like putting key in apartment door (his wife
doesn't have this key). I like the unreal plastic feel of the
desktop; it's not like *furniture*. I like the way the chair grabs
my back. I like how the typewriter keys jump at the touch of
my fingers. I like the feel of paper. I like licking stamps and
envelopes. I like the taste of mucilage. (Unless there's an
awful lot of outgoing mail—a pun—I never use that water-
fed sponge. I'm my own sponge, as he's his own octopus. Like
him, I salivate without bells.)

—Most of all I like taking dictation, being one among
millions who hold medium soft pencils poised over steno-
graphic pads balanced on soft thighs. I like being a multi-
millionth part of One, listening to the Universal Voice. U.V.
dictates, I respond. It is not humbling to join him thus: UV/b.
No, the upper and lower case, separated only by that falling
fence, are again "precious segments of a poem." I respect Him
Who Dictates as I respect her who takes dictation. And even
more, HIM WHO DICTATES to Him Who Dictates. In his
journals, for instance, where I see dictation within dictation. . .

—*I dream of being naked while I work, so nothing comes
between me and the dictation I receive, so I don't miss the
raw caress of a single word. I guess this must be every writer's
dream.* (This was not italicized originally. I went back, be-
neath the words, underlining them, imagining how they would
look when printed in italics: frail and vulnerable, tipped
slightly to the right.)

—Nor is it humbling or self-effacing to admit that I could
not have invented, say, that lyrical opening whisper of his and
yet was able to take it down. . . . The words that start as his—
or hers—become ours. Ultimately they belong to all of us. I
say, as he says, *"Imagine*, a sense of property about words. . . "
For me, it is enough to hold the key to this apartment and its
files, closets, drawers. . . to control even temporarily the copies
of letters, memoranda, articles, drafts, notes, whispers. . . sup-
plies. . . raw materials. . . . Things cross my mind as they cross
my desk.

—I like my job. It keeps me from going out of my
mind. . . . I wonder if he will fire me if my book is published.
Do writers distrust writers, as businessmen do? Will my
years with him (my weeks of listening closely) become a blank
in my résumé? There's that possibility, and the other: that
when you leave a job or a character, *you* are firing them. Per-
haps I know this man (this composite of so many for whom
I've worked) as well as I want. And this wife also, Mrs. Aver-
age Reader. And those kids, smaller fragments of me. . .
Why further stretch any of these relationships? Like him, I
know that they are infinitely expandable; like her, that they
must end. . . . Like him, like her. . . . Why not tune in on other
voices? I'm not Edel or Painter, and he's not James or Proust.
If I were a biographer, I'd've invented Mrs. James and Mrs.
Proust. I'd've spun the dial in my mind until I found them. A
single life is impossible for me to imagine, frightening,
whether at Lamb House, Rye or in a Paris cork-lined room;
but especially in New York, the most impossible city in which
to be alone and the only one where everyone is. Here we're
alone at rush hour on the subway, and in line for a movie, and
waiting for a table at a restaurant. Our only constant company
is money. With it we buy tokens, tickets, tables. . . We buy

hellos. . . . I wonder what I'll do with *their* hellos, his and
hers, if in the future they interrupt my taking dictation from
someone else. I want to say goodbye. I want *them* to say good-
bye. . . . Good buy. Another pun. . . .
   —I read, I read, I read. Yes, next to shopping I like
reading most. Buying books is one answer to two needs. . . .
Best of all I like books about authors, fat biographies like
those of James. . . Proust. . . Joyce too. . . . I like those quiet
lives, those small whispers within cosmic whispers. . . yes, yes,
yes. . .
   —I heard him say of words: "They should be carved in
stone or cast in bronze, MADE PERMANENT WITH EF-
FORT." For a moment he was no longer whispering, but
almost shouting to emphasize the weight of stone and bronze,
their preciousness. Yes, words should be treated as a costly
commodity, not thrown away like so much carbon on the pulpy
pages of a spiral-bound stenographic pad. As I move circu-
larly from page to page, I pretend sometimes that I am writ-
ing on vellum. I count sheep. Every word, every page is a
matter of life and death. It's no wonder monks illuminated
their manuscripts; they knew their work was sacred—their
stenography no less than His dictation.
   —I'm reminded that my pad is the product of once living
trees, if not of sheep. And yet I know it's a dead thing resting
on my knee, the cool green cardboard cover turned in, the
white sheet cooler still beneath sharp corkscrew teeth. . . .
Alas, correspondence is mostly routine. Like him, too often I
have that sense of reality only waste can give. I am his accom-
plice. I squander words on the page.
   Like him when he was picking up the voices and images
of enthusiastc editors, in my mind the interview continues.
Whispers (or whatever its ultimate title) will be published. I

will be public. *We* will be public. The interviewer will ask
one last question:
"If all you do is take dictation, who's dictating now?"
"One of me," is all I can reply. Another approximation.
I type up all the dictated notes. It's a long letter, even if
not so long as the one she received from him. Arbitrarily, I
finish, as dictated, "Very truly yours," pull the last sheet from
the typewriter, and wait for a signature—or signatures.

mine: #2

Dictation, yes. All arts are performative—and, to some extent, secretarial. I accept no theoretical hierarchies, no elitist distinctions. To play the writer is no better than to play the actor and to be part of the cast no better than part of the audience. Roles are equated, roles are switched. We fight for our seat in the orchestra or balcony as for our places on stage. Wherever we are we accept dictation—only that, even if the message is to resist. Dictation—yes, yes again, the will of the unconscious.

New York awakens. It glows as it pulls back its blanket of smog. I hear the city clear its throat, feel the traffic grow heavy, watch street lights go out and office lights turn on, listen to the first murmurs of revolving doors. . . . My eyes roll down the avenue, past too many banks.

Today, as one intermediary dealing with another, I will deliver this book to my agent. I will give him this open letter to the world, to myself. . . . I have finally signed it, though I insist that their signatures, hers and his, should have been beside mine—neither above nor below but beside. . . . And still I hesitate. I wonder if I shouldn't place it in a stamped self-addressed envelope and assure its safe return to me. I would like to send it into the world, without risk, neatly packaged, and to have it return unseen by other eyes, unheard by other ears.

I will begin my walk, holding the package tight, pretending someone might want to steal it, yet knowing that if this happened it would be because the thief thought it contained something more valuable to him than words.

As I walk from block to block, past anonymous and synonymous buildings, through this living cellular city which destroys and rebuilds itself, I will not relax my grip. Even knowing better, I'll be anxious, tense—uptight, they say now. The drivers of cabs, trucks, busses, private cars will shout at each other and at pedestrians, and the pedestrians will shout back at them, and the cops—rookies and veterans—will shout at the drivers and the walkers and those who only stand and wait.

What would earlier singers of this city think of it now? Melville? Whitman? James? Crane? And what the writers who came as tourists? Mayakovsky? Céline? Lorca? Would they agree that the city has fulfilled its secret promise? What do I think? Was the promise, there in the hum bouncing between Rockefeller Center and Wall Street, lost now in the screech of a siren? Was it there in the ticking of clocks and the tinkle of small change, and lost now in the electronic chorus of giant computers?

There is anger in the air. Hostility is an aspect of pollution.

I had thought there was really no such things as waste, that what was wasted remained within a closed system, with matter being converted into energy and energy into matter but nothing being destroyed. I had thought our resources as endless as love and, like love, not reducible by loving. And I had thought that, as with money, there was no limit to the amount that could be issued. I was wrong on every count. Waste no

longer seems so satisfying, nor so jolly and amusing. We can
no longer afford the extravagance of Busby Berkeley produc-
tion number, Broadway musical, or TV spectacular set on the
moon—not when they're played with our lives, our air, our
water, our space, our quiet.

There are newspapers everywhere, spilling out of gar-
bage cans onto sidewalks and into gutters and down the streets.
The newspapers are no longer symbols as in 'thirties movies.
They are not simply scraps of the past blowing away. They
are not lives . . . crushed, soiled, torn . . . ultimately destroyed.
No, they are—as they always were, except when treated as
art—printed news: birth announcements and obituaries, a
record of winners and losers, reports on the weather and the
theatre, and and and and and and and, a million conjunctions.
. . . The newspaper implies tomorrow as much as it records
yesterday. It is a product of some giant rotary press—a sort
of primitive TV—an endless loop of images always changing
but neither getting better nor worse. Tomorrows are time's
children, and as with any child (she said) the gain and loss
don't balance out. We can't trade nature for technology. (She
said too, "Isn't it mostly an eye for a tooth and a tooth for an
eye?")
They bickered for first look at the *Times* and I recorded
their bickerings (along with her ughings and ichings). Now,
like Ruby, I silently read the *News*. There I can follow the
stories of individuals; the *Times* writes about nations. There
I hear whispers; in the *Times* I hear lectures. Perhaps the
Times contains too many words, a waste of words. . . I struggle
in its sea of ink which will eventually form the very words that
pass judgment on these words of mine. (Critics take dictation
too, but from evil gods.)

Yes, my errand is run, my tale—circular and old—is told. I will hand this package of pages, these pages of words, to my agent and wait patiently for . . . what? A receipt? A recycling? Further dictation? I will wait, not knowing why, knowing only that I have no choice.